UNFORGETTABLE CHILDHOOD

Unforgettable Childhood. Short Children's Stories for Grown-ups. ©2025 Olya Yarosh. Translated and revised from the Russian language version published in Europe. All rights reserved.

ISBN 979-8-3492-0329-9

All Scripture quotations, unless otherwise indicated, are taken from the Holy Bible, New International Version®, NIV®. Copyright ©1973, 1978, 1984, 2011 by Biblica, Inc.™ Used by permission of Zondervan. All rights reserved worldwide. www.zondervan.com The "NIV" and "New International Version" are trademarks registered in the United States Patent and Trademark Office by Biblica, Inc.™

Scripture quotations marked HCSB are taken from the Holman Christian Standard Bible®, Copyright © 1999, 2000, 2002, 2003, 2009 by Holman Bible Publishers. Used by permission. Holman Christian Standard Bible®, Holman CSB®, and HCSB® are federally registered trademarks of Holman Bible Publishers.

Scripture quotations marked (KJV) are taken from the KING JAMES VERSION, public domain.

Scripture quotations marked (NKJV) are taken from the NEW KING JAMES VERSION®. Copyright© 1982 by Thomas Nelson, Inc. Used by permission. All rights reserved.

Scripture quotations marked (AMP) are taken from the Amplified Bible, Copyright © 1954, 1958, 1962, 1964, 1965, 1987 by The Lockman Foundation. Used by permission.

Scripture quotations marked (NLT) are taken from THE HOLY BIBLE, NEW LIVING TRANSLATION, Copyright© 1996, 2004, 2007 by Tyndale House Foundation. Used by permission of Tyndale House Publishers, Inc., Carol Stream, Illinois 60188. All rights reserved. Used by permission.

Scripture quotations marked (OANT) are taken from The Original Aramaic New Testament in Plain English by David Bauer.

Scripture quotations marked (NASB) are taken from the NEW AMERICAN STANDARD BIBLE®, Copyright © 1960,1962,1963,1968,1971,1972,1973,1975,1977,1995 by The Lockman Foundation. Used by permission.

Scripture quotations marked (NCV) are taken from the New Century Version®. Copyright © 2005 by Thomas Nelson. Used by permission. All rights reserved.

Translation by Vera Mishchuk
Illustrations by Alla Badsar

Olya Yarosh

UNFORGETTABLE CHILDHOOD

Short Children's Stories
for Grown-ups

Bright Books, 2025

CONTENT

Thank you 9

Foreword. Time is of the essence 11

Introduction. A bouquet of forget-me-nots 13

Olya. Ikebana — Homework for
Dad and life lesson for his Daughter 21

Ari. Surprise! Inherited Joy 29

Nelya. Daddy's little girl (princess). 37

Katerina. Give away your own Birthday 47

Leah. Loyalty soaked from childhood. 55

Julia — How a Grandfather Gave
His Granddaughter a House of Worship 65

Vasily. Invisible thread to a Mother's heart 73

Irina. An Easter surprise for the children 83

Paulina — Scars: A Reminder
of Her Sons' Unique Destiny. 91

Taya. A Mother's Love². 99

Vera. Buckwheat for 100 rubles 107

Pavel. Croup, asthma, and tarsal coalition 115

Sasha. Make a wish 125

Katie. Mangoes and flip flops 133

Marina. A heart melting Dress 141

Conclusion A Happy Childhood —
the Second Chance 149

DEDICATION

*I dedicate this book, first and foremost, to my dear parents —
Pavel and Nadezhda Okara — they were creators
of my happy childhood.
My heart is filled with gratitude towards you!*

•

*I also dedicate it to our children — our son and two daughters.
Paul, Katerina, and Arianna, your dad and I are ever
so thankful for the privilege and pure joy of being your parents.
Every one of you is a special gift we have waited
and wanted so much.
My heart is filled with love for you!*

•

*I also dedicate this book to everyone who
just became a parent or maybe you have been raising
your children for some time now. We — their parents —
are the creators of their childhood.
My heart is filled with faith!
With God's help we can create their happiness!*

•

THANK YOU

I am forever grateful to my Lord for His perfect love and grace towards me, His daughter.

•

I am grateful to my husband, Vasily Yarosh, for his love and support and his faith in me. In you our children have the best dad in the whole wide world — thank you for your love and kindness.

I am grateful to my treasures — my blessings from the Lord, my son Paul and my daughters — Katerina and Arianna. You are my inspirations, my constant joy and my loudest cheerleaders. I love you with all of my heart!

•

I will never cease to admire my parents, Pavel and Nadezhda Okara. I will be forever grateful to you for our happy childhood, for your example of a strong and healthy family. Thank you for introducing me to my Heavenly Father and sharing your wisdom through life by example.

•

Thanks to my sisters, Vera, Anna, Irina, and Anastasia — my closest best friends, my brothers Sergey and Alexander, and to all my extended family. Your love and support is priceless.

•

Thank you to all my friends, our church family, and to everyone who continues to inspire me with their lives lived by example. To the people who continue to add flowers to my bouquet, making my life so fragrant — I thank you!

•

And a special word of gratitude to the translator and editors of this book; Vera Mishchuk and Grace Duyn — thank you!

•

FOREWORD
Time is of the Essence

Everyone comes from childhood. Although some seasons of our life can be "skipped over", left out, even consciously avoided, when it comes to childhood, it is inescapable. Everyone's childhood is their own and very different. Starting from the cradle, we perceive the world around us uniquely and very differently, and teen years leave a deep imprint forming and dramatically altering our views about the world. Some children reach adulthood faster than others, skipping over college years by immediately plunging themselves into the workforce. Others spend years in school, getting their education. Still others may go back to school to finish their degrees as middle aged adults.

Some couples step into parenthood in their 20's, others in their 40's, and still others perhaps never. Everyone's life experience is uniquely different, including their childhood.

Our early years are essential, albeit short compared to the rest of our lives, and begin as a clean slate — a period of gradual discovery of our own selves and the world around us.

Even if the initial trajectory of our life is corrected over time, childhood events will have lasting implications. Our past experiences can shape us into the best or worst parents for our own precious children, whom the Lord has entrusted to us.

This book is written about children, but it is intended for adults; for those whose childhood, though left far behind, is at the same time ever so close.

Childhood is far, relative to the number of years left behind, but close — because we always carry its imprint in our hearts. All our memories, impressions, and emotions return as we relive the moments of joy and delight, or pain and resentment, again and again.

Some of these experiences we keep on the surface, readily sharing them with our children and friends; others are buried deep within us in the dark corners of our memory and we carefully avoid anything that might remind us of their existence.

Some events of our childhood may seem neutral, mere facts about life — the way things were back then, in that city, that house, that family. But nevertheless, these seemingly unimportant things also have their influence, not only do they shape our self awareness, but also how we will raise our children in the future.

Each person is like a chrestomathy — a collection of childhood stories.

A storybook — and as we read through its pages, we learn what is worth imitating, and what things we need to protect ourselves and our children from.

INTRODUCTION

Stirring our own memories. What are the most vivid memories from our childhood? Is it the joy, the pain, the tears?

What is it that has stayed with us forever? And how does our heart choose which memories to throw away and which to keep and cherish?

Our early memories get sifted in ways we cannot comprehend, leaving only the brightest moments for us to keep like a bouquet of forget-me-nots. These memories never fade — because they become part of us forever.

Childhood is for growth — for growing *up*, and not only in a physical sense; more so in a spiritual sense; our souls grow upwards, reaching higher, towards the light, towards heaven — upwards towards God.

Every child's soul reaches for its Creator, it nourishes itself with everything that is of God: His love, affection, tenderness and care. And from the moment of birth we are drawn to people who possess this kind of divine love. We yearn for it seeking its source; some will find it in their childhood, others only later in life, often through making peace with their own childhood.

Divine love, as well as its absence, leaves a permanent mark within our souls.

After all, love is like air for our souls to breathe.

Years will pass, but these outbursts of God's love will never fade, on the contrary, as we cherish these memories they only become brighter; and we will carry this divine love forward, from our past to the present — to our own children.

· OLYA ·

Ikebana — Homework for Dad and a Life Lesson for his Daughter

Olya is a second grader in a typical soviet school, and is already taller than many of her classmates. A skinny girl with piercing green eyes, peering from beneath her evenly trimmed chestnut bangs, she is smart and perceptive. She is wearing a plain brown dress made of prickly wool trimmed off by a beautiful white collar and cuffs — a classic soviet school uniform. Her apron, the same color as the highlighted details on her dress, is perfectly ironed. And although Olya lives in an ordinary soviet city, her father is highly unusual. He is a christian, the head of a large family and a faithful servant of the Church during difficult times of the soviet government's persecution.

One day in the middle of the school year, when the windows were covered with frost, but there was not much snow on the ground, her teacher, Yulia Pavlovna, described Ikebana to Olya's class. Ikebana is the Japanese art of making bouquets made of fresh and dried flowers, as well as other natural materials.

The teacher explained the idea to the kids, showed them some beautiful pictures and, dividing the class into small groups, gave them a group project as homework. In a week's time they were to bring their ikebanas, made from similar plants and materials, to school.

I guess one has to admire the teacher's "creative approach", as it would seem that this simple project placed a heavy burden not only on these eight-year-old kids, but also on their "poor" parents.

Now, to set the stage, I must say a few words about the Rostov region's landscape where Olya's family lived. The middle stretch of Russia is a never ending wilderness, in winter it looks gray and bare: low growing shrubs, leafless maples and sleepy birches are the only things growing here. From the fruit bearing varieties: apples, apricots, and cherries grow here. Evergreen trees are not found in this region. Therefore, the kids had a perfect opportunity to showcase their imagination and creativity with this project.

The due date was fast approaching and on the very last day, the kids, not finding any beautiful twigs in their neighborhood, decided that someone must venture outside the city to a nearby Agroforest. Rumor had it that there you could find rose hips and red berry bushes, and that even in winter their branches would still have berries on them. Surely they would make for the best looking bouquets. The kids looked at each other and then fixed their eyes on Olya. Everyone knew her dad had a car — the red "Lada", which they jokingly called "The Penny".

In Russia's bitter winter daylight is short, and it gets dark very early. When Olya came home that day, she asked her dad to go with her out of town to look for dry plants.

Most likely, her dad did not even understand the meaning of "ikebana", but by the looks of his eight-year-old daughter it was clear: the matter was urgent and important. In addition, his daughter made a convincing argument: if she fails to collect these materials, she will let her classmates down and will get a bad grade.

During that time, Olya's dad worked two jobs to provide for their large family. He also served as a worship leader in their church and that took a lot of his time. If that wasn't enough, he was constantly worrying about his youngest baby boy, who was recently diagnosed with an incurable disease. This completely exhausted and overworked man taught his daughter one of the most valuable lessons in her life — a lesson of love. A child is not only important to her parents, but also what happens in her life is just as important. After all, against the backdrop of constant parental concerns, problems all around, and an endless "to do" list, this ikebana looked miniscule and complete absurd.

But Olya's dad started "The Penny", warmed it up, and as evening fell, together they arrived at Agroforest, a small patch of low growing trees and bushes sparsely covered by snow that lay right behind the Pioneers Camp buildings. Olya asked her father to drive a little closer and off the road. They stumbled about the frozen rut — the frozen over autumn slush, trying to find any materials suitable for her craft. But all they managed to collect was a few twigs with partially fallen dry and twisted leaves on them, that resembled a broom and looked nothing like a bouquet even when not put together. It was apparent that just a few months ago, all the berries were collected by their town's "babushki", grandmothers, who put them in jars up into the pantries and down into their cellars. But at least she had something, that was good. After a short deliberation, father and daughter decided to supplement this bouquet of sticks with something from home. Absolutely frozen, they happily got back into "The Penny" and her father started the engine, but the wheels skidded off the snow covered ground and the car would not move.

For the next hour, her dad would chop branches with the ax he had wisely brought from the house, putting them under the tires, and trying again and again. The car was still stuck, making the tracks deeper and deeper. Late evening was gently replaced by the darkness of winter's night and there was not a single soul in sight. The roadway was completely deserted and inside "The Penny" a frightened eight-year-old girl was clutching a sad looking bouquet with her stiff frozen hands. But her dad didn't panic. He kept throwing armfuls of branches under the wheels until the car jerked forward and finally drove out onto the road.

Pressed by guilt and regret, little Olya carefully studied her father's face. It seemed that now her dad would tell her everything he thought about this project. But not a single negative word fell from his lips, no moralizing about how this whole thing could have turned out or how important it is to do everything in a timely manner. The head of the family just drove his daughter and her "bouquet" home, as if nothing had happened.

They arrived back home, back to their familiar surroundings. They went back to tea with pancakes, and small children laughing and crying. Back to frequent and uninvited, but always welcomed guests. Back to the sounds of music and homework late into the night, and life went on.

Thirty-five years later, Olya does not remember what that ikebana looked like or what grade she received in her nature class. But that cold day is forever seared into her memory, when her dad set aside all of his plans just for her. And most importantly, Olya will not forget the feeling that overwhelmed her from head to toe, the warm feeling of significance and love shown to her by her father on that trip.

LIFE LESSON

•

Sometimes important things appear insignificant to adults.

But Jesus himself said about the children: "...whatever you did for one of the least of these brothers and sisters of Mine, you did for Me" (Matthew 25:40).

Christians talk about big things: about ministry and serving God.

But what does the Lord Himself require of us?

What in the end will be "counted worthy"?

Surely it won't be grand projects or performances, because sometimes it is the small simple things done with love and to "the least of these" that count the most.

Of course reading the Bible with your children and praying together is important.

But it is also important to simply play with them, to answer their requests, or to go biking together with the whole family. Or maybe allowing them to invite their friends over for pizza. Or taking them to the park.

Remember the words of Jesus: everything that we do for the next generation with love is indeed done for Him.

FORGET-ME-NOTS

•

"God is able to bless you
abundantly, so that in all things
at all times, having all that you need,
you will abound in every
good work."

(2 Corinthians 9:8)

· ARI ·
Surprise! Inherited Joy

There's no secret that every student dreams of school to be over! Shortly before spring break, kids in every classroom began to share their exciting plans for the week, or rather, their parent's plans for this long-awaited week in early April. Some gloat over their promised trips to Hawaii or Florida, others are dying of envy, and others are silently watching everyone, just happy that now they can finally get enough sleep and play a lot of computer games.

Arianna's family had been planning this school break for a while. This summer her parents were planning a big trip, so during a family meeting they decided that in the meantime, they will spend spring break at home. There were so many ways to have fun staying right where they were! They had so many parks nearby, and four bicycles in the garage. School ended on Friday, and on Saturday their cousins came for a sleepover. On Sunday they all went to church as usual. Officially, Spring Break started on Monday!

Sunday evening, Arianna's mom suddenly started doing laundry, which was completely unusual for a church day. She worked late into the night, folding the kids clothes all by herself, which was also strange. Before everyone went to bed, the parents announced their plans for the next morning. First, everyone would sleep in, then they'll have brunch at their favorite cafe — a French Bakery in downtown. Everyone loved the idea, and the kids peacefully fell asleep anticipating the beginning of a long awaited Spring Break.

Morning came with not a single alarm going off at 6:30 a.m. All five alarm clocks were turned off, though it is still not clear why both mom and dad had their own separate alarm clocks set for the exact same time, but because of that Monday morning began pleasantly and promisingly. The girls were picking their outfits, asking mom what they should wear, dad was talking to someone on the phone, and when everyone was ready, he announced that on their way to a cafe they would have to take grandpa to the airport.

Ari's grandparents lived nearby, so after a short side trip they were on their way. The kids were getting hungry and annoyed by the unexpected detour. Naturally, they started whining, "It's eleven o'clock! Soon it might rain, and then we won't be able to go for a walk at all!"

The airport was about twenty minutes from home, and during the whole ride Ari's mom and dad were discussing their grandfather's upcoming flight to Los Angeles, as if deliberately teasing the kids with all the glorious details, "Amazing! Only an hour and a half on the plane, and you are no longer in grey and rainy Portland. After such a short trip you are in warm, sunny California under the palm trees!" They kept talking about their previous visits to the City of Angels, her mom and dad enthusiastically listing the attractions they had visited there before, knowing full well that their children, who had never been to Los Angeles, still had to wait a few more months to see the sun return to damp Oregon.

The car stopped at the "Departure" entrance , but grandfather was not in a hurry to get out. Suddenly, mom turned to the children and asked, "How about instead of sending grandpa, we fly to Los Angeles instead?"

"Let's do it!" Dad answered her without thinking twice.

"This is not funny!" the kids responded angrily. "Let's just go to the cafe already, we are so hungry, we can't stand it!"

But their parents seemed to be having too much fun with their joke. They both got out of the car and said, "Come on, we have this whole week free! Let's fly to LA and have some fun in the sun!" He then opened the trunk and pulled out three small suitcases.

Perhaps it is always this way, the younger the child, the faster they believe things. The older kids, not understanding what was happening, kept asking, "What do you mean? Now? Where are the tickets? We don't even have our things packed! This joke is too cruel! We won't be going anywhere this year!" Three pairs of confused eyes stared at their parents. The two older teenagers, bewildered and doubtful, expected this joke to have a twist of some kind. But the youngest one, Ari, lit up with faith and excitement that burst out with tears of pure joy.

One second later she was tightly hugging dad around his neck. It looked as if she was about to strangle her father with happiness.

Their grandfather said his goodbyes and took their Toyota home. Two happy adults and three surprised children stood under the sign for their airline. Dad handed everyone their tickets that he had printed out at home. Mom assured the kids that they will find everything they'd need in their suitcases carefully folded by her. Now everything fell into place: the strange "laundry day" on Sunday evening, sorting things out until late into the night. After going through security, they all had their breakfast in a cafe right before departure — everything as promised.

A few days later while sitting by the pool, under the hot sun and tall palm trees of Palm Springs, Ari once again hugged her parents and said with pure delight, "You know, this is the best surprise in my whole life! When I grow up and have kids, I will make one just like it for them!"

The entire week, Ari's parents were basking in their children's pure joy and gratitude. The photos they took at the airport were proof of that. Ari's mom would forever keep these memories in her heart and in these pictures. The spontaneous mini-vacation that was made possible by a sudden discount on tickets turned out to be three times cheaper than a trip to Hawaii. But to this day the children remember it as their most favorite vacation ever.

LIFE LESSON

•

Not only do the most painful and tragic events leave a deep mark in our memory, but the vivid and unexpected memories leave ones too. So, don't be afraid to surprise and delight your children!

This is akin to God's Grace, when we receive something unexpected and undeserved.

Nowadays, more than ever, benefits become privileges and quickly shift into the category of "must haves". What some can only dream of, others take for granted. In modern terms, today's parents have a much better quality of living than previous generations: our children have access to what no one else has had before. The opportunities are endless. Yet, the degree of how spoiled, arrogant, and demanding, or, how grateful, humble, and appreciative our children will grow up to be, rests entirely on us — their parents.

You can provide extravagant vacations, traveling to the best resorts many times a year, yet it will fail to leave a single trace of gratitude in your children's souls. Or you can surprise your child with something much smaller than a spontaneous trip to California, and they will remember it for a lifetime.

Because the size of your gift is not what matters, not the trip itself, or the ice cream, but the rush of positive emotions. The children never forget moments like these.

FORGET-ME-NOTS

•

"...all this is for Your benefit, so that the grace that is reaching more and more people may cause thanksgiving to overflow to the glory of God."

(2 Corinthians 4:15).

· NELYA ·
Daddy's Little Girl

Beautiful, colorful, and slender with piercing blue eyes. Openhearted and sincere. Today, Nelya is a daughter, a pastor's wife, a loving mother to three young men and their wives, and a grandmother to Rose, a beautiful baby girl.

As a child, God revealed Himself to her as a tender loving and caring Father.

For Nelya, one of her most vivid childhood memories is a strange episode when her father would not buy her a doll.

When she was about five years old, they lived in soviet Ukraine. She vividly remembers how she walked into the store, "The Children's World", while tightly holding onto her father's hand. The little girl was a copy of her dad, both had the same deep blue eyes. She also possessed his impeccable taste for design and the love for all things beautiful.

There on the shelf she saw two full size dolls: one with long black hair, the other one was a golden blond with a bob-cut and freckles on her beautiful, painted face. She had a tag attached that read, "Walking Doll." If you were to take this blond beauty by her left hand, she would start walking alongside you.

Little Nelya pleaded with her dad: "Please Daddy, please buy it for me!" But her dad said, "Oh no, it is too expensive. It costs 11 rubles**, we can't afford it!" But the little girl could not take her eyes off the beautiful doll. Seeing how much his daughter wanted this toy, dad offered to buy the other one — her cheaper sister. She would only cost 8 rubles. But the long-haired brunette was not a walker, and Nelya really wanted the doll that could walk.

Having exhausted all of his arguments, dad resorted to a "nuclear option".

"Just look," he said. "This doll is definitely not a Christian. Look at her, she's got short hair and makeup. Why would you want a toy like that?"

Now, you have to understand that back then, forty years ago, in the long forgotten Soviet Union, a Christian could be seen from afar, not only for their faith, but also for their appearance. The Christian women of Soviet Union dressed in plain, modest clothing. They never wore makeup or nailpolish, and would usually style their long hair by putting it up in a bun and covering their heads with a chiffon scarf. The men likewise dressed neat-

---

* [Ruble] a unit of Soviet currency. The average soviet workers salary at the time was around 160 — 180 rubles.

ly, modestly and plain. One could easily spot a baptist or a pentacostal christian out of the crowd by their distinct appearance.

Father and daughter left that store without a doll that day, but nevertheless, the little girl took the doll with her, her image imprinted itself onto Nelya's heart as an unfulfilled childhood dream.

From time to time Nelya would still think of her, even after many years. When one of her own sons would ask for a toy, a car or some other thing, the doll and the events surrounding that day would suddenly reappear in her memories, flooding her soul with strange feelings asif carrying her back in time. Nelya would always ask her husband, "Please, let's buy it for him. I don't want him to have the memories like I do with my doll."

Years passed. One time she asked her aging father if he remembered this story. Her dad said yes, and admitted that he was so taken back by it. He remembered that after they returned home Nelya cried all day long. Her dad could not understand what was it that stopped him from buying that doll. He asked his adult daughter to forgive him, for causing her those bitter childhood tears. But Nelya held no resentment against dad. She simply wanted to understand why this doll would not leave her alone. Soon everything became clear.

Unlike most soviet children, Nelya was fortunate enough to be born into a christian family who raised their children in the christian faith, knowing full well that, at that time, this was not only shameful but dangerous.

The little girl believed in God from early childhood. But, even having once experienced a divine connection with the Lord, we continue to encounter Him for the rest of our lives, each time ever more deeply. All of eternity will not be long enough to fully comprehend our Creator, so infinite, so boundless, so endless in His wisdom.

One of the most important revelations about God that everyone must receive is the understanding that the Lord is our loving Father. Moreover, the Lord is our Creator. Savior. Friend. Mentor. Teacher. Advisor. I think everyone has experienced, when words and events suddenly become the missing pieces of the puzzle, unforgettably and deeply revealing God's truth to us, but in a new and unexpected light of the soul and the spirit. This kind of revelation is called the "inner knowledge".

In 2010, together with her family, Nelya imigrated to the United States, where on summer weekends, the residents open up their garages, selling their unwanted stuff for pennies on the dollar. You can find "anything you never needed" at the garage sales: paintings, dishes, strollers, bicycles, books, skiis — in short, everything including the kitchen sink. Sometimes you can find strange souvenirs brought from abroad or gifted by tourists, who bought them for their loved ones. We all know what happens to those useless things, they get put away up in the attic until the time comes to pull them out and put them up for sale. Most garage sale finds are miscellaneous things, but sometimes one can find a real "treasure", that is if the previous owners have misjudged its true value.

On one such warm Saturday, Ilya, the youngest of Nelya's sons, begged her to take him to the neighborhood garage sales. He was hoping to find something special. A big surprise awaited them at their very first stop.

Nelya stepped out of the car and immediately saw HER.

"It's her!" she yelled in amazement. The boy looked straight ahead but saw no one except the large doll standing beside the table. "What are you talking about, Mom?".

"It's a toy from my childhood!!!" Nelya literally yelled out and ran to look closer at her. "It's the same exact one, just like that doll from 'The Children's World'!" She thought to herself. Only her tag was in English: "Walking Doll."

Nelya took the doll by her left hand, and just like 30 years ago the blond with freckles on her painted cheeks began to walk next to the elegant thirty-five-year-old woman.

It was Dejavu. Nelya stood with a doll, and her Heavenly Father was there right besides her. God was looking at His daughter with love and broadly smiling, speaking to her heart, asking, "Well, is that what you waited for?"

Now her son Ilya was begging his mom to buy this doll for herself. But she felt ridiculous, "I'm a grown woman, why would I need a doll?" But it was too late, her son had already bargained with the owner and they agreed on a price. That day the mother and son returned home with a doll.

Nelya placed her in the middle of the room and plunged back into her usual household chores. Later that night, when everyone was asleep, she began to reflect on that old story with the doll and suddenly she heard the voice of her Heavenly Father.

That night she didn't go to sleep until the morning, but the heart to heart conversation she had was so needed, not only for herself, but also for her friends and those she serves today.

Because this story is not so much about the gift but of the Giver, about our Heavenly Father, who spoke to Nelya on that night saying: "If I remembered this toy — a doll I knew that you once liked, if I care about the pain and tears of that small little girl, do you really think that years and circumstances can hinder the fulfilment of My will? There's nothing too difficult for Me!"

LIFE LESSON

•

Perhaps our Heavenly Father wants to show us, parents, that all the hard work we do to take care of our children, fulfilling their dreams and desires — is all good. But our main task must be elsewhere: it is much more important to teach them who is the True Source of our health, wealth and wisdom.

Yes, we strive to do our best for our sons and daughters, however, it is much more important to introduce them to God, who wants to have a personal relationship with them. God our Father does not become our children's "Grandfather", to the contrary, they are also His children and the Lord wants to bless them with their own unique "gifts" that we mere mortals do not possess. Sometimes He even turns back the clock, to reach back and present us with something special from our childhood, reminding us again and again, that at any age, even as grown adults we will always remain His little children.

FORGET-ME-NOTS

●

"See what kind of love the Father has given to us, that we should be called children of God; and so we are..."

(1 John 3: 1).

"... for your Father knows what you need before you ask."

(Matthew 6: 8).

· KATERINA ·
Give away your Birthday

How can one teach a child to embrace generosity and loving care for others? Most will agree that this can't be done by words alone. This task requires something bigger and much more substantial.

But what exactly?

Will simply setting a good example in hopes that they will follow it be enough? And what if you were to create a situation that would encourage your child to sacrifice something of great value for the sake of others?

"No, no you can't do that", some parents would say. "That is pure manipulation!" In some ways, that is true, because this approach risks violating the sacred boundaries of your child's autonomy.

On the other hand, some parents consider this method a good deed; on account of our human depravity and sinful, selfish nature that is totally unwilling to give anything of itself to others.

Katerina is the first born, the oldest girl in her family. Her mother eagerly awaited the birth of her little girl and celebrated each and every month of her pregnancy. When she finally arrived her parents were overjoyed.

In a year's time and thanks to breastfeeding, little Katyusha, as they lovingly called her, became a chubby cheeked baby, with cute rolls all over. In honor of her first birthday, mom dressed her little girl in a cute pink dress with a matching hat, an outfit fit for a real princess! For this joyous occasion guests were invited and a birthday cake was made. Her parents opened the gifts and thanked the Lord for giving them this blessing, their baby daughter.

Time flew by.

Soon it was Katerina's 12th birthday. By now this sweet, kind hearted big sister and mom's little helper was in middle school. She was absolutely indispensable around the house, helping her mom with dishes and laundry. And her mother would often joke that she now had two pairs of hands in the kitchen.

Shortly before her birthday party, Katerina shared her ideas with parents, who she wanted to invite and what to make for dinner. Their family usually celebrated everyones birthdays at home, although some of her friends, who were from wealthier families, celebrated theirs at a cafe or a bowling alley.

That same spring, a new girl started coming to Katerina's church. A single dad would sometimes bring her with her younger brother and sister, and sometimes church members would pick the children up and bring them to church. No one had ever seen their mother. Some said that the woman had become addicted to drugs and left her husband with three small children.

The girl seemed shy, quiet, and withdrawn when adults were present, but was the total opposite in the company of her own peers, turning into a daring and uncontrollable child.

That same spring their church launched a Bible School course for middle school children. Classes were held every Thursday. The kids absolutely loved everything about this Bible course: the lessons, the games and prizes, the food, but most importantly, they loved hanging out with their friends. Katerina together with all her friends and the new girl were all enrolled in it too.

It just happened that that year, Katerina's birthday fell on Thursday. When someone had a birthday, the teacher would leave a few minutes at the end of the class for a little celebration. The whole class would stand in a circle and pray for the birthday girl (or boy), then the kids would blow out the candles and receive gifts. Katerina couldn't wait for her Thursday.

At the beginning of that week they suddenly learned that the new girl's birthday was that same week only on Wednesday. And looking at her teenage daughter, Katerina's mom decided that she was now old enough to experience "real joy", the kind that comes from giving rather than receiving.

The Bible says: "...it is more blessed to give than to receive" (Acts 20:35). But this truth is incomprehensible in theory, one can only grasp it through personal experience.

So, Katerina's mom shared an idea she had with her daughter, "What if we were to plan a surprise for the new girl? She would never suspect that we knew about her birthday. What if we were to buy her presents in advance and at the end of your class we would bring out a cake with candles for her and say, "This is all for you!"

Katerina listened patiently, thinking how she could do the same thing but not on her own birthday. "Mom, sure it's a great idea, but can we do it on some other day? Maybe we can take the girl out to a cafe. She is new and she doesn't even have friends at the school. Or, let's do it on her own birthday. Although, I don't know how to get everyone together on Wednesday, but maybe we can do it without everyone. How about we will congratulate her on everyone's behalf and give her a nice gift. And just think, how will I explain your plans to all my friends? They're all waiting for my birthday party and they probably won't like this whole idea!"

Her mother gently began to explain that "sacrifice" is most often uncomfortable, hard to achieve, and even painful. She began to explain that "by giving away something that is rightfully ours to those who need it the most, we are putting aside our own desires and wants." Feeling contradictory is absolutely normal, because it sheds light on our internal struggle between our spirit and the flesh, between our "wants" and our "want nots".

To one degree or another everyone experiences this. In the end, that which we desire most wins, but acquiring stuff rarely leads to "real joy." Katerina listened carefully and hesitantly agreed to "give away" her upcoming birthday to the new girl. She immediately ran off to message all her friends that they should also bring a small gift for the girl.

When that long awaited Thursday had finally arrived, Katerina's mom stopped by the store on their way to church. Katerina wrapped a birthday present for the new girl.

At the end of class, all the kids gathered in the center and her mom said, "You all know that today is a very special day for my daughter Katerina, it's her birthday. But instead, we will celebrate the birthday of the new girl even though it was yesterday." Standing surrounded by classmates, the girl was slightly confused. She could not believe in what was happening. A minute later a cake with candles was brought in and everyone began to sing, and then pray for the girl. Katerina gave her the gift and hugged the birthday girl. All her friends did the same thing. Just then, the girl covered her face with her hands and burst into tears of pure joy, happiness, and love from the attention she received in that unforgettable moment.

Katerina's mother also cried. She was overjoyed and happy for her daughter, who was able to give sacrificially and graciously. Her mom's heart was in tears both from overwhelming compassion towards the new girl and from overwhelming gratitude to God for all these kids.

LIFE LESSON

•

Sometimes we need to nudge our children in the right direction, helping them to step outside of their own comfort zones, stepping outside of their own "self", so that they can experience pure and real joy of sacrificial love and generosity. The joy that overwhelms your soul when someone else is experiencing happiness.

Encouragement is just as important as setting an example.

FORGET-ME-NOTS

•

"And let us consider how to stir up
one another to love and
good works"

(Hebrews 10:24).

· LEAH ·
Loyalty soaked from childhood

In the fall of 1962, little Leah, along with her mother, two younger sisters, and four little brothers, went on a long and treacherous journey — to a far away and bitterly cold Siberian wilderness.

The young mother, utterly exhausted and together with her seven small children, spent one whole week on the train car traveling to the city of Tomsk. In total they spent — one hundred sixty eight (168) hours in a crowded train car, "obshiy vagon"*, to be exact. They were traveling to be reunited with their father,

---

* [Obshiy vagon] — was a high occupancy, open seating train car that did not have assigned seating, the usual 54 paired benches were occupied at will. The carts original intent was for short distance travel, but during soviet rule, poor travelers would utilize its low fare for traveling as far as the Sivberian GULAGs and back.

who had been a pastor of a small church, but was sent into exile after serving his prison sentence for his faith*.

The Soviet Union considered all religions to be a crime and harsh penalties could be enacted for those caught practicing religion. His crime was precisely that, and he had been sent to exile in Siberia. The grey city, buried under a thick layer of snow, met them with bitter frost. Snowdrifts piled high so high above their heads they resembled mountains, and the cleared sidewalks were like a giant maze with walls taller than people. Here Leah's mother and the children were welcomed by the Orlov family — their brothers in the faith. They stayed with them for a few days, and then went on to their final destination — the small village of Molchanovo, lost somewhere among the swamps of the Tomsk region.

There were only two ways of getting there, in the summer by a boat via river Ob, or by a car but only in the winter, when all the swamps would freeze over with a thick layer of ice. The children, being small and not understanding all the dangers of their upcoming trip, enthusiastically piled up into the back seat, with their mother and the baby sitting next to the driver.

Little Leah would never forget this trip. It was 200 kilometers, almost eight hours of driving on poor road conditions and deep snow drifts made the car jerk from side to side. The children became car sick and would vomit to exhaustion. From time to time, the driver would stop to let them catch their breaths. Pale and

---

* The Soviet authorities deemed all religious practices illegal and punishable by harsh penalties, including those of confiscation of property, imprisonment, exile and even death.

exhausted, they would literally fall out of the back seat right on the roadway and lay with their faces into the snow. After they felt a bit better, the car would continue on. They were driving towards bitterly cold frozen winters and the swarms of mosquitoes in the sweltering Siberian summers — to a life in a filthy unfurnished barracks.

Of course, their mom could have waited for their dad to come home from his exile, many other wives of christian ministers whose husbands were serving sentences in Siberia for preaching the gospel did just that. She could have at least left her youngest children with their grandparents, sparing them from that treacherous and dangerous journey, and from becoming practically homeless, moving from one small apartment to the next.

But for Leah's mother this was a matter of being "faithful" to her own husband and to her children. She believed that the family must always stay together no matter the circumstances.

Having gone through such difficult trials, together with their mom, her sons and daughters soaked faithfulness into their souls, but not from their mother's words or moralizing, but through her personal example. They lived out faithfulness together and became living witnesses to God's miracles — the Lord took care of their large family, providing for them and guarding them through it all by sending them help through complete strangers.

Yet these lessons they had learned were not conveyed to them through eloquent speech, but by the living example of their parents' daily lives. Looking at their life, the children saw the power of their inner strength and their unshakable faith, that triumphed over fear and doubt, a faith manifested and verified by faithfulness. They soaked in their parents' faithfulness through the air, by absorbing it through the atmosphere around them.

Years had passed. The children grew up and created their own families.

Beautiful Leah met her future husband when she was 17. The young man was tall and handsome. They quickly fell in love and married. Shortly after they held a healthy baby, and were blessed with two more. Over time, silent and undetected, a venomous serpent crept into their house; he slithered gradually hiding behind everyday chores and the worries and cares about the kids.

This cunning foe, a skilled assassin of every human paradise, employed a strategy that was as old as the world itself. Like a green genie from the bottle, this serpent also slithered out of the bottle. Only this trickster would not fulfill anyone's wishes, but rather would leave destruction in his wake, trampling hopes and dreams, and by his devilish embrace slowly choking the life out of a once-strong and healthy family. For many years Leah's husband was held captive in this suffocating grip of neverending drunkenness, irresponsibility, and disease.

Hopelessness, pain, poverty, fear for her children, and dread of the unknown crept into once happy household gripping the heart of a young mother. As if her heart was bound with iron chains.

Yet, she continued to birth more and more children. It seemed that ,for her, all hope for any kind of normal life should have died a long time ago. But Leah would not give up.

She continued to be faithful to her God and to her husband, the husband who in his drunken stupor would fall asleep right on the street in the middle of the cold frozen winter. If he was out too long, she would go looking for him, she would find him and drag her drunken husband home. Then she would wash him, warm him up and nurse him back to health.

Leah's elderly mother would often come to visit her daughter. Together they would pray and cry, cook and clean, and weed the garden beds. If it weren't for that garden, they would starve.

Meanwhile the alcohol slowly drained the life and health of her husband. Neighbors, friends, and relatives only sighed in sympathy, making it clear with their heartfelt remarks that no one would condemn her if she took the children and left. The serpent himself would cunningly whisper these thoughts into her ear, hoping to totally demolish their family, trampling her children's future underfoot.

But with all her strength, the young mother resisted that fate, because she could not doom her children to become fatherless. She firmly believed in God's faithfulness, and she was certain He would help to take care of them.

Looking at her own mother, Leah saw the faithfulness of the Almighty, which she herself soaked in from childhood. Remembering that filthy train car, and how they huddled with their large family in cramped barracks that housed the exiles, she understood what a great price her mother paid for all of them to be together with their father.

A wife will not abandon her husband.

That was out of the question. Leah would not abandon him to the enemy and she prayed him out from alcoholism addiction. She battled the cunning serpent and won her husband from his captivity. After he had repented and was freed, the man became completely different: he was now loving, caring, hardworking, and successful. Together they rebuilt their house, opened their own business and now enjoy life surrounded by their children and grandchildren.

Leah's daughters grew up to be true beauties, inside and out. One after another they all got married and went off to live in different cities, even countries. Each of them had their own unique journey in their first years of marriage, their own struggles and misunderstandings, difficulties and even illnesses, everything that is inherent to any union between two very different people.

Her daughters are still very close with their mother. And whenever they call her to ask for advice, the answer they hear in reply is a gentle reminder to remain faithful to God, their husbands, and children. The truth that their mother, the little girl named Leah, soaked into her soul sixty years ago and faithfully carried through her whole life.

LIFE LESSON

•

How can children not only adopt, but also put into practice those rare and noble qualities their parents posses?

In my view, this can't be learned by simply hearing about such qualities or viewing them from a distance. It is essential to live out real difficulties together with mom and dad; overcome obstacles, become eyewitnesses to how they overcome struggles, sometimes even be forced to fully participate in making the right decisions, and to do noble deeds.

This is precisely the way noble character is absorbed by the children, brick by brick laid into the foundations of their lives. And one day their future families will be built on that foundation.

We can only pass on that which we ourselves live out. Without real live experiences, our "message" to the future generation is empty.

The apostle Paul instructed young Timothy: "…and what many witnesses have heard from me, then tell faithful people who would be able to teach others as well" (2 Tim. 2: 2).

This young man was a faithful disciple of Paul. Like a son he followed his teacher everywhere. Timothy soaked in the virtues of his mentor, and was able to pass those qualities to the other believers, they in turn learned from him and were able to carry them further and further.

The young disciple was also a witness to Apostle Paul's daily living practises and his lifestyle. Because simply hearing the words is never enough, the truth must be accepted and imitated in order to be passed on.

Our lives depend on it. We are not called to be meer observers, couch potatoes trapped by social media. Our goal is to showcase Christianity in practice, inspire and develop our children by example, and faithfully encourage their gifts so that they can give unto others that which they themselves possess.

FORGET-ME-NOTS

•

"... but what I do have I give to you ..."

(Acts 3: 6).

"... and what you have heard
from me in the presence of many
witnesses entrusted to faithful men,
who will be able to teach
others also."

(2 Tim. 2: 2).

· JULIA ·
How a Grandfather Gave His Granddaughter a House of Worship

Before World War II, in a little village called Ogorodniki, 35 kilometers from the small town of Kalinkovichi in the former Soviet Socialist Republic of Belarus, an elderly couple was building a house. An ordinary, sturdy house, with one grand bright room and a Russian masonry stove in the middle. They were building it for their daughter, who was married to Joseph Yarosh.

In the meantime, their daughter and her husband lived in another village nearby. They came to visit her parents often with their children Julia, Volodya, Anya and little Vasya. Grandfather loved the oldest daughter, Julia, the most.

Life in the village went on as usual with never ending house chores, feeding the animals, and the backbreaking work in the fields and in *kolhoz**. But it also had its own joys. Simple things like warm homemade bread, fresh milk, the smell of hay, and the endless green fields.

Maybe it was the exhausting work (just to put food on the table), or the harshness of a life void of toys and treats, that influenced this elderly man to give little Julia a present not suited for a small child.

One day, the grandfather, driven by some unknown reason, suddenly got up and said, "Julia, what if I give this house to you?" He took a piece of paper and wrote out a "gift certificate" putting the name of his granddaughter up top.

Life went on and everyone forgot about the old man's generosity. The sheet of paper with his granddaughter's name layed untouched, hidden away for many years.

Then, the terrible year 1941 came. World War II reached Belarus, enveloping it in a dense fog of fear. The rapidly advancing enemy stormed the towns and villages, forever changing the lives of its people. Julia's father was taken to the frontlines, and never returned. Later, relatives managed to find information that somewhere far in the forests of Siberia, "Private Joseph died as one of the braves". They never learned anything more about him.

Her mother was left a widow with small children in her arms. Most of all, she was afraid of the German occupation. Her fears turned out to be well founded;the enemy's army was advancing closer and closer. One day, the door of their house swung open from the blow of a soldier's boot — men in Nazi uniforms stood on their threshold. Shouting loudly in German and not caring if they were understood by the poor woman, they gestured to the door, demanding she leave, for that night they would be staying in her house. With no time to take anything with her, the mother and the children ran into the forest, just outside their village, where their prudent father had prepared a dugout right before going off to the front.

Morning came and Julia's mother thought to return home to grab a few necessities, but, coming to the edge of their village, she saw thick smoke and flames rising from the place where their house once stood. This was the thank you the grateful German visitors left behind in their merciless wake. The night before, Julia and her mother brought in fresh hay and densely covered the floor with it, so the fire broke out in seconds and the building could not be saved.

How can they survive in that cold dugout without any food or clothes? Julia's mother took her children and walked to her parents' house. There they received the army notice informing them of her husband's death. Julia's family survived those horrifying years of war by sticking together. But just as the worst seemed behind them, a typhus epidemic gripped their village. First, Julia's grandmother and grandfather came down with the disease, then her mother too. The grandparents were terribly weak, they had barely survived the war and simply could not fight the illness, so they both died. Her mother was very sick. She was feverish, completely incoherent, and violently shaking. They took her to the village hospital.

People say, "When it rains — it pours", and although the war was finally over, the suffering of the common people did not end. The country needed rebuilding. Through organized collective farms (kolhoz*), the Soviet government tried to replenish its dwindling food reserves using the hands of their utterly devastated and crippled farmers.

So, while their mother lay dying in the hospital, the children were ordered to immediately vacate their house to make room for the newly appointed collective farm chairman. But where would they go? Back to the cold dugout?

There was no one around to plead on their behalf. By then Julia was a bit older, she was enrolled in school. As was expected of the eldest, she took full responsibility for her younger siblings.

She suddenly remembered that strange moment when her grandfather in an outburst of love gifted her his house. She searched for the "gift certificate" in her grandfather's things. After she found that piece of paper with her name on it, she boldly knocked on the door of the Village Council's office. Adults looked at the paper then listened to little Julia. Because of her grandfather's random act of generosity, that document ensured the house was theirs to keep.

Thankfully, their mom got well, and was discharged from the hospital.

---

* Kolhoz — a Collective Farm — the result of soviet collectivism in agricultural farming. In the 1920s the government seized land and equipment from rural farmers and forced the peasant class to work on its collective farms, where the majority of workers did not receive a cash salary, their labor was measured in "work days worked" that was then traded for food and meer necessities..

But before everything was finally settled, something truly life changing happened. Something that will become decisive in their future happiness.

Their mom had fully recovered, but she returned home a completely different person; she told the children that, according to the doctors, while she was utterly delirious, hanging between life and death, she kept running somewhere. The medics had to tie her down to the bed. But it turned out that while delirious with fever, in agony, she saw the horrors of hell, which she could not unsee. Nightmares continued to torment her even after recovery, until her sister mentioned something about the Christians who happened to live nearby.

In the end, Julia's mom became a Christian and discovered that hell is a real place. Purgatory is not imaginary, but she did not belong there. She took her children to the house church and after a while she opened the doors of her own home to become a place of worship. And that is how a sturdy little house, in that small village, built by the loving hands of Julia's grandfather for his daughter, and gifted to her in a spontaneous gesture of love, became a House of Prayer.

Today, Julia's youngest brother, Vasily Iosifovich, is 85 years old. He survived World War II, the famine of 1947, and buried both of his parents. He still recalls his life with tears, for it was marked with unimaginable suffering. But the story of their house became his solidifying moment, it was not just a vivid childhood memory, it was a genuine miracle that he saw happening right before his eyes, the miracle that had forever grounded his faith in the Lord.

LIFE LESSON

•

In life there are no accidents, or, as they say, accidents aren't accidental.

All of us, fathers, mothers, and grandparents, need to be sensitive and intuitive. Often our feelings aren't just our imaginary desires, but rather the voice of the Holy Spirit, who knows the future, and is preparing something special for our children (through God's providence).

We can not see into our future. An old proverb says: "Hope for the best and prepare for the worst." Unfortunately, the future is out of our hands, but we know the One who knows everything about our future. The God who loves and cares for us, and gives us the freedom of choice. We can either cope with what will happen on our own or we can listen to His voice. But, the voice of the Holy Spirit is subtle and gentle. Some people mistake it for their own intuition, some even boast about their insightfulness. Others find many excuses and rationalize the reasons why they shouldn't pay attention to a sudden desire to do a noble deed. But those who listen to the inner voice, even when there is no clear understanding of the reasons "why", yet, in hindsight will understand. In those moments, they will see the hand of God.

FORGET-ME-NOTS

•

"... And your ears shall hear a word behind you, saying, "This is the way, walk in it," when you turn to the right or when you turn to the left."

(Isaiah. 30:21).

· VASILIY ·
Invisible Threads to a Mother's Heart

Every newlywed couple dreams of starting a family, but life dictates its own rules. For some parents having a baby doesn't come easy. The following story is about such parents.

For Vasily and Antonina the birth of every child was a genuine miracle. For years after her wedding, the young woman could not conceive. Many tears were cried and countless prayers sent up to the heavens. Her doctors advised her to change climates, so the couple moved to another city. She finally gave birth to two sons. They still wanted more children, but after years of painful waiting, all hope seemed lost and they made peace with the fact that they would only have these two boys.

When both Vasily and Antonina were well over forty and their hair began to turn grey a miracle happened — the Lord gave them a third child. His parents nicknamed him — "сын старости"* — "son of our old age."

Life went on as usual. Vasily and Antonina worked at the same factory but on opposite shifts; little Vasily's older brothers were fully enjoying their teenage freedom, and he was left to his own devices.

The family occupied a small apartment on the ground floor of a nine-story tall residential highrise, in a suburb that was called "Baburka", a newly built industrial area at the birthplace of the infamous soviet made automobile, Zaporozhets. From their apartment's balcony you could see both the kindergarten building and the school, encircled on all sides by identical concrete apartment highrises.

All of these buildings were densely populated by children, whose parents tirelessly worked in the auto industrial factories of the city of Zaporozhye. At the end of their long work days, tired parents would pile into overcrowded trolleys to return home, stopping along the way to get a fresh loaf of bread at the local grocery store. When pay day came, everyone would buy live fish that was brought and still swimming in a huge yellow barrel, fitted on the back of the dump truck.

Right before dinner time, the highrise would fill up with the aroma of freshly fried fish. For little Vasil'ok, as his mother affectionately called him, fish day was the best day of the week and he would eagerly wait for the next week's feasting.

---

* "сын старости" — "son of our old age" an oldfashion nickname older parents use in slavic church culture when referring to their young children.

After his mom would wash the dishes, she would lay down to rest on the sofa. With her little boy sitting next to her, snuggling his skinny body against hers, he would lay there completely still listening to how her heart was beating.

For as long as he could remember, his mom was always sick. She suffered from diabetes, high blood pressure, and heart disease. Losing his mom was his scariest and ever present fear; it haunted him constantly, even in the middle of the night, turning his dreams into nightmares. Sometimes Antonina would fall fast asleep on the sofa, and to little Vasiliy it would appear that she has stopped breathing. Utterly horrified, he would shake her until she would begin to soundly breath again. So great was his anxiety, that he was afraid to fall asleep, because it seemed that he was in charge of guarding his mother's heart and keeping it from stopping.

When Vasiliy was 5 years old it was time to start kindergarten, and although the building was right in the middle of their courtyard, he could not tolerate being separated from his mother. One day the caregivers called his parents telling them that their son was missing. Everyone panicked and searched the entire facility, but the boy was nowhere to be found. A few hours later he was found at home, under the bed. It turned out he climbed in through the open window on their balcony.

It took some time, but Vasiliy got used to his teachers and his new friends. Then he started school.

By that time his older brother married and began building his own house. His parents would rarely come home, they were working long hours and helping their son with his house, and then there were church services; they didn't have enough time for it all. But Vasiliy was never bored: he and his friends made every nearby construction site their personal playground; a dangerous, but very exciting adventure! When he was 7, he was "taught" how to swim by his comrades. They simply pushed him off the cliff into the rough waters of the river Dnieper. Together with the same friends, Vasiliy explored every single beach in the vicinity of Zaporozhye. Sometimes they would catch a ride via slow moving cargo trains that would take them along to their destination.

Several summers in a row, his parents sent their youngest son to visit his uncle, in Sukhumi, a beautiful city on the Black Sea. He spent the hot months with his cousins, collecting glass bottles along the beach and cashing them in to buy shish-kebabs and his very first bottle of Coca-Cola. The boy was independent, to say the least.

Together with his parents Vasiliy and his friends attended a Christian church. When he was a teen they organized a church orchestra and later started a worship band. Vasiliy taught himself to play the double bass. As a graduate, at 18 years of age, he decided to move to Kiev (the capital city of Ukraine) to enroll in Theological Seminary. His parents did not oppose his move, though they did not fully support him either. Vasily's dream became a reality when he graduated with a bachelor's degree and opened a Bible School.

A few years later, while in graduate school, he met his future wife. They were married at the age of 26. But the youngest son would finally introduce the love of his life to his mother long after the wedding.

After the birth of their first child, the couple moved to America, where Vasiliy's parents came to live. By age thirty, their youngest son already had three children of his own. He actively served in a local church, ministering and preaching together with his wife. Life turned out beautiful.

Vasily's parents now lived nearby and visited more often than the kids came to visit them. It seems that the elderly parents needed these visits more than their young and very busy children. Running through the everyday hustle and bustle, Vasily would remind himself about his duty to his parents — to call or visit his mother. The little boy who had once snuggled against his mother's chest making sure that her heart would not stop beating was now a distant memory. He was a grown man, the head of a large family, now clinging tightly to his own children and listening to their breaths.

But still, despite all the changes, he still deeply cherished the gray-haired old woman who birthed him. When she would have heart problems, in those moments, the darkness would envelop Vasiliy once again, reviving his greatest childhood fears of losing his mother. Overwhelming emotions would come over him, reminding him of that ragged old sofa that stood in their Baburka apartment.

Antonina always asked God for this favor, for her to leave this earth in her sound mind and without pain, and to not be a burden for her children.

One day she had a massive heart attack. Death came instantly, but the paramedics managed to start her heart again, and she was then placed on life support. A day later, after fervent prayers of her loved ones, the doctors concluded that there was no sign of any brain activity and that her life support should be turned off.

Doctors gave time to the family to say their goodbyes and left the room. Suddenly, Vasily realized that in the next few minutes his mother's heart, carefully guarded by his love, would stop beating. And this thirty-five-year-old grown man wept, tightly clinging to the body of this elderly woman exhausted by illnesses, he cried loudly and bitterly.

In that moment, from within his soul, a little boy screamed with a grown man's voice, "Momma, please, don't leave! Don't leave me, Momma! "

His wife could not fully comprehend the depth of his suffering and despair. Seeing the pain of her beloved husband was almost unbearable. She tried to hug him, as if to remind him, "You still have all of us, our love." But she stopped short and quietly stepped aside.

Then came the most difficult moment for Vasily, it was time to let go. He entrusted his mother into the hands of the Lord, and from then on he did not shed a single tear, not even at her funeral.

Her youngest son knew where she belonged, the pain of separation no longer tormented him.

Later that day, in the evening, Vasily and his wife had a deep conversation. They recollected their childhoods, talked about the business of life and how short it is, and how invaluable the time spent with family. Suddenly, his wife candidly admitted that because of all his independent childhood stories and adventurous youth, she had no idea how strongly he was connected to his mother, so much so that she could not even imagine that he would react that strongly to her passing. "I've never experienced such deep pain, I literally physically felt the spiritual threads between us tearing, and my connection to her heart being ripped apart, letting go felt unbearable." Vasily explained to his wife.

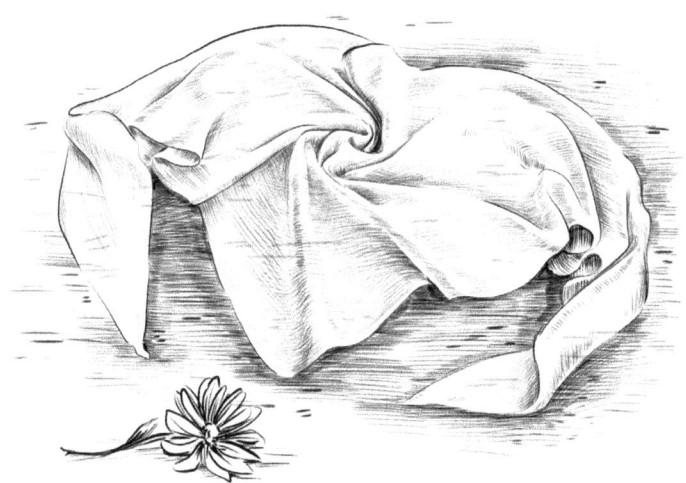

LIFE LESSON

•

For most parents, undoubtedly, until their dying breath their connection with their children is very similar: the spiritual ties of unconditional love are everstrong, like thick ropes, able to withstand any hardship and overcome any separation.

But the children who are grown adults also experience these ties. They are living by their parents' blessing, by their love and prayers. You can live miles apart, seldomly calling or coming to visit, but nevertheless, this changes nothing. The emotional connection with a mother and father does not dissipate, it is not subject to time and space. This connection is like a foreshadowing, like an archetype of the Greatest Love in the universe, that is both our Father and Mother — the Love that keeps us in this life and will keep us in the life to come "... through all kinds of mutually fastening bonds" (Eph. 4:16).

We should not underestimate the emotional bonds between parents and their children. Better yet, our own attitudes towards our parents will lay a foundation for our own children setting an example for their future.

God gave us the opportunity to strengthen these bonds, but we also need wisdom to make sure that the bonds of love would not break prematurely, but also would not turn into chains tying adult children down.

FORGET-ME-NOTS

•

"Honor your father and your mother,
that your days may be long in the
land that the LORD your God is
giving you..."

(Exodus 20:12)

· IRINA ·
An Easter surprise for the children

It was 1995. Just three years earlier, in a small city in the Northern Caucasus mountainous region, an urban church plant was born. And although this was an entirely brand new congregation, it was bursting full of life.

After the fall of the Soviet Union, the winds of newfound freedom swept over the country. Many people, especially students and academia, developed a thirst for God and an openness to the Gospel. Young people repented alongside senior citizens and were being baptized, becoming disciples, and caring forth the Great Commission — bringing faith to the nations.

The pastor of this church lived in a small provincial town nearby and drove to the church office almost daily, bringing his family along several times a week, his wife and four younger children, all of them under the age of 10.

An Officer's House Hall with beautiful marble steps and red velvet chairs was rented for church services. But, like in any other rented hall, before each meeting all the equipment had to be set up and connected, all the classes for Sunday school set. At the end, all of this had to be cleaned up, and everything in the hall put back in its place. Because of this the pastor and his family came to the services long before it started, and stayed long after everyone had left.

Sunday after Sunday, his wife and kids sat in the car for several hours while her husband still ministered, talking with people, checking to see if they had forgotten anything, and only then they went home. The pastor's wife often would bring sandwiches with her, and sometimes she bought Viennese buns in a cafe around the corner, knowing how long it would take to get home. So, while sitting in the car, eating sandwiches and pastries, they were developing a very useful quality that is very helpful in life, patience, the fruit of the Spirit.

And there was always a long line to speak to the pastor. Some people had no idea that the pastor's tired and hungry family was waiting for him. But others who knew thought it was no big deal; they could wait, after all this is their ministry, their voluntary sacrifice.

People of all walks of life came to the church, some very skeptical and biased, others on the contrary, fully sincere, opening their hearts to the Lord and even inviting their christian brothers and sisters into their homes. One such precious soul was Anastasia. She always came to church without her husband, alone. The woman was very wealthy, she lived in the center of the city in a spacious apartment with high ceilings.

That spring, before Easter, she came up to the pastor's wife and invited the whole family to a festive dinner after the service. The children got very excited, hot homemade food is much better than a couple of hours in a car even with fresh, but already pretty boring Viennese buns or sandwiches.

Easter service, as always, was very long and festive, full of uplifting words, joyous songs and children's poems. When it finally ended, the pastor and his family drove to Anastasia's house. As they walked into her expensively furnished apartment, they saw a huge table set and beautifully decorated in the middle of the room. Its sheer size was so impressive that the guests' first reaction to the hostess was a surprise: "Are there more people coming?"

In ordinary Soviet apartments, only a few people could fit at the dining table, so the children were used to eating separately, sometimes sitting on the couch.

As it turned out, Anastasia was not expecting anyone but them. Yet, when arranging the chairs, the hostess gave each child their own seat, which immediately made the children feel welcomed.

But their biggest surprise was a large vase, standing on the smaller table, filled with large branches. On them, new buds were barely peeking green leaves. And every branch was decorated with a Kinder Surprise chocolate egg that hung suspended on red ribbons. This bouquet was not part of the Easter decorations, but it was standing there for a reason.

Anastasia bought these delicacies for the children for dessert, and each of them had more than one Kinder. The kids had never seen this kind of treat before.

Of course, they were used to being treated to sweets, but this kind of imported treat, like toys brought from abroad, were very expensive. At that time, during post soviet depression, every single child dreamed of a chocolate egg with a hidden toy inside. And here there were dozens of them! The children were overjoyed with this gift. They would cherish the memory of that day for a lifetime; the pure love and kindness shown to them.

Almost twenty-five years later, far away in Washington State, on one beautiful Sunday morning, two rambunctious boys, barely awake, joyfully shouted a greeting they had memorized for this day: "Christ is risen!" and "Risen indeed!" Today they would be going to church, where they would sing in the children's choir and recite poems together with other children.

The youngest, Anton, was only 2.5 years old, and had memorized two poems — both his own and his brother Mark's. Four-year-old Mark, with big smart eyes and long eyelashes, was very worried that his younger brother would mix up the poems and recite his instead of his own.

Their mother smiled to herself, as she was changing her newborn boy, thinking about the surprise she had prepared for the children. Judging by the sound of bare feet running on the wood floors, they were running to play downstairs. Suddenly, there were the sounds of ecstatic joy from below.

The beautiful table in the dining room was topped with a large vase with branches cut from a tree in their yard, with the new buds just beginning to peek little green leaves. And on every branch hung a chocolate treat , Kinder Surprises. It all was for them!

Irina sent the photo of her boys next to the vase to her close friends. When they asked, "Where did you get such an original idea?" She simply answered, "It's from my childhood."

This is how decades later, and across continents and oceans, Anastasia's branches sprouted with Kinders. They took root and grew into a tree that produced good fruits: love and kindness to the children.

LIFE LESSON

•

Don't forget about your children. The Lord Jesus spoke more than once about a simple glass of water for the man of God and about its reward. Perhaps the reward lies precisely in this, that any work done with love — is eternal. This process is endless, because, as we touched the hearts of our sons and daughters with kindness, even by simple treats, we perpetuate an invisible mechanism of kindness that will touch all the children whose path they will cross in their future. It's hard to say which one of today's branches will grow into a tree. But, as we know, everything earthly will pass away, but that which is eternal — lasts forever.

Once, in the middle of His journey, Jesus rebuked His disciples who were trying to restore order: "Let the little children come to me and do not hinder them ..." (Matthew 19:14).

Christ paid attention to the littlest ones. In the midst of the service, He laid His hands on them and blessed them, giving us this example. As parents we must do the same often.

What you have done to one of these little ones, they will eventually do to their little ones. This statement is unfortunately true even on the opposing end.

May the Lord help us, open our hearts, not only for the children we birthed, but for all; making their lives overflow with goodness through our ministry; and in turn they can pass this goodness onto their own children, saying with a smile, "This is from my childhood."

FORGET-ME-NOTS

•

"... Truly, I say to you, as you did it to one of the least of these My brothers, you did it to Me."

(Matthew 25:40).

· PAULINA ·

Scars:
A Reminder of Her Sons' Unique Destiny

A young mother of two rambunctious kids, was busy preparing dinner. Time seemed to pass slowly. All of her Mondays, Tuesdays, and Thursdays looked the same: she said, "Goodbye," to her husband in the morning, then spent all day tending to the children. Somehow between their naps and play time she would try to manage to do all the household chores, and finally greet her husband with a smile after the hard days work.

Paulina had two children. Her oldest son was 4 and her baby daughter was just 8 months old. The kids would be up early in the morning, and with them, the whole house became alive. Breakfast was prepared for the children, diapers needed changed, warm hugs were given to soothe their cries, and a million questions about everything in the world were answered.

When she was in her teens, Paulina became an orphan. Back then the state would separate the children in her circumstance, but her older sister applied for custody of her younger siblings, and so they were able to stay together.

When she was just 18, Paulina met the love of her life and married him. During their first years as a couple, their family size doubled while their financial life was only slowly improving. Now, there were four of them. They rented a little old house in the center of a growing town in northern Washington state, that stood on the grounds of a local Lutheran church.

One day Paulina was just about finished making borsch, a traditional slavic soup made with cabbage, potatoes, and red beets. She was putting the last ingredients in the pot: shredded cabbage, dill and garlic, setting the timer for five more minutes — and lunch is ready! Mouthwatering smells filled her tiny kitchen. Meanwhile, her baby daughter was running around the tiny room in her walker, crashing into things, and getting stuck on the furniture. She would call for her older brother's help with her cries.

Then tragedy struck. A horrific accident that left scars on her little boy and a deep wound in the hearts of his parents forever.

No one is ever prepared for tragedy — disaster is always unforeseen.

Somehow, the stove in that little old house was not secured to the wall, as is required by safety standards. Everything happened instantly. The lower oven was turned off, but for some reason it's door was open. The pot with boiling soup stood on the front burner, and little Serge was standing next to his mother. Her baby girl pushing with her strong feet, rolled around in her walker and ran straight into them. Little Serge, being wise beyond his years, held out his hand to stop his little sister, and simultaneously put his other hand and his whole body weight on the open door of the oven. The stove tilted and the pot with boiling soup tipped, spilling its boiling contents all over him.

In mere seconds tragedy forced its way into their lives, destroying their familys' happiness and quiet rhythm.

The little boy's back, shoulders and arms were severely burned. Burns covered almost half (40%) of his body. The first few days were spent in a local hospital, where all his dressings were changed under general anesthesia. As it turned out later, the child was injected with a mega dose of painkillers, which caused severe life threatening side effects.

The reaction of his small body to the medication was so unpredictable that everyone immediately forgot about his burns. And now the doctors were fighting for his life. No one gave any guarantees that he would survive this. It seemed that their night had suddenly become even darker, and their nightmare turned into unspeakable horror.

Paulina and her husband tried their very best to hold onto hope, trusting in God in the midst of the storm. They begged Him for help, cried, whispered through the tears, and when they were utterly exhausted for words they silently moved their lips, asking the Lord for mercy. God listened and drew near. The Good

Shepherd tightly held them by the hand, and He carefully carried their little boy close to His heart.

Little Serge was transported by a plane to the Regional Burn Center, where the Lord sent them the very best specialist, who promptly made the right decision to carry out the operation.

Back then, extensive burns were treated with shark skin transplants. This procedure worked well, but as the child grew he would constantly need repeated surgeries. A skingraft from a different part of the body would be considered an ideal option, apparently a painful and complicated procedure, but it would spare the need for future surgeries and leave less scarring.

Through a veil of tears Paulina watched the doctor as he measured little Serge's arms and shoulders, and then marked off the areas on his legs and hips, from where they would get healthy skin grafts for his transplantation.

There's no need to share the details about what the little boy looked like after the surgery and what it was like for his parents to see him like that. But we must pay tribute to their courage and faith in God and sheer tenacity. Most likely, young 20 something Paulina had no idea that a mother's love can tap into the endless source of strength, patience, love and hope.

But the moral of this story is a little different.

The boy eventually recovered, and the terrible nightmare of his suffering has faded into the past. But the scars remain present both for him to bear under his clothing and hidden deep inside the hearts of his loved ones. Yet, the wounds of the past no longer bleed or burn. Being reminded of what had happened, his parents are not tormented by the meaningless questions like, "Who is to blame?", "For what?", and "Why us?".

Years passed. Paulina's children got older, and like in any other family, the teen years were a bit rocky.

I think most parents worry about their children and about decisions they make — wishing them only the best. They wish for their children to know the Lord, to find their calling and to be happy in life. Today, his almost invisible scars constantly remind Paulina of God's mercy, His love and kindness.

Perhaps someone else would tell this story as a grave tragedy that destroyed the life and happiness of this boy and his family. Perhaps someone would stumble and lose faith in God. When tragedy strikes, people often become depressed and blame themselves for what happened.

But not Paulina!

For this young mother, the scars left behind on her son's body are a visual confirmation that the Lord prepares a unique destiny for her boy. She will never forget the events of that day. It is no accident that God brought her child back to life. His scars are like a sign and at the same time a reminder of his destiny.

With these words, Paulina continues to inspire her now grown son. She believes in the Lord with all her heart and no longer lives with the pain of the past. Today, Paulina worships the Lord believing that her children have a special calling from God.

LIFE LESSON

•

Our children's character is largely shaped by our own reactions. Self-pity, victimhood, and offence can become foundational; shaping wrong attitudes towards the difficulties we all must face through life.

May the Lord protect our children by granting us the wisdom to face every challenge in a way that would portray truth, as well as God's grace, that He has given onto us.

FORGET-ME-NOTS

•

"And we know that for those who love God all things work together for good, for those who are called according to His purpose"

(Rom. 8:28).

· TAYA ·
A Mother's Love[2]

Moscow, the capital city of the Soviet Union at the time of its downfall, had vast food shortages and extreme poverty of ordinary people.

Fourteen days before her son's first birthday, his young mother gave birth to his brother — her second child. She was pregnant for two whole years, as her children were born so close together. At that time, simply finding groceries was difficult, so no one had good nutrition. People ate what they managed to get and vitamins were nowhere to be found. As a result, her second baby was born prematurely and with a birth defect: weak legs. Time passed, the baby grew, but even at eighteen month he could not stand on his feet. Different doctors, including those from the children's clinic, made the same terrible diagnosis — "rickets", leaving them with a hopeless prognosis: most likely, the boy would remain confined to a wheelchair. He would never walk, run, or play football.

For some, the word "diagnosis" is equivalent to a life sentence. But not for everyone. Some are unwilling to give up, they continue to fight, seek, and knock on doors. And for those who knock, as the Lord says, the doors will be opened, and those who seek shall find (see: Matthew 7: 8).

A mother's heart is capable of tapping into unlimited divine reserves of power. And yet, there is another kind of love that is like the mother's — the love of a grandmother.

Val's grandmother's name was Taya. Her love for her grandchildren resembled a mother's love, but to the order of magnitude — love^2. Not only did she fully support her daughter, but she would also stand in the gap for them.

In those years, his grandmother worked at a food storage facility at the Government's Retreat Mansion, where the Soviet government officials came to vacation. One time she came to the head doctor of that institution and told her about her grandson: she talked about his diagnosis and his grim future. Taya spoke of her little grandson with such passion and love that the doctor whose name she can no longer remember, was moved with compassion for her. Taya wept bitterly, and poured all of her pain onto this Georgian woman. The doctor was deeply moved by her grief, even though she never met the boy personally.

The doctor did not cry of lament, she simply reassured the grandmother with these words: "Taya, don't cry. We will do everything in our power. " And then she gave her completely non-medical and perhaps not even professional advice, "Your grandson needs specialized nutrition — black caviar".

This advice was like being told to get a rock from the Moon.

"Thank you doctor! But this wasn't funny. Putting the baby on a black caviar diet, when finding sausages is practically impossible?! Where would one find this exquisite delicacy, moreover — how can his poor parents afford such a thing?" Taya thought.

But the head doctor was not joking. She not only knew what to do, but she knew how it could be done. Her responsibilities included prescribing and distributing food products for the Government Mansion. There's no secret that the Soviet governments nutritional requirements for themselves were very different from ordinary citizens. Black caviar, an unattainable delicacy for mere mortals, was on the daily menu of senior government officials. At the risk of her own high position, and even freedom (such things were punishable by law), the doctor decided to write off a certain amount of caviar every week and deliver it to the sick boy by a spesial courier. The driver brought this medical treat still wrapped in its packaging.

Today, it's hard to imagine what risk this woman took. She held a fairly high position, which guaranteed financial stability and wealth for her and her family. If someone were to find out about what the doctor was doing, she could be fired from her prestigious job, and that's in the best of circumstances.

But a mother's heart cares not only for her own children. It feels compassion and love for other boys and girls, sometimes doing extraordinarily brave things for them!

The caviar was written off, and the courier delivered it to Taya's address in Kuntsevo. Every day, Val was given a spoonful of black caviar with additional baby food brought from the same warehouse.

And with each time a car secretly arrived at their house, hope and faith in his full recovery grew stronger.

Several months passed. The baby's legs got stronger, and he began to recover. Soon after, Val took his first steps; it was very late for his age and completely unbelievable for his diagnosis. His parents have now forgotten how long this delivery scheme lasted, but his first healthy photograph was as a well rounded cheeky four-year-old boy with a double chin firmly standing on his feet.

Val started school together with his peers. He began to play sports, his favorites being wrestling and running. After graduation he acquired a profession, started his own business, and got married.

Today he's raising two sons, and two daughters, cute blue-eyed blondes. With God's help, Val stands firmly on his feet today, in the full sense of the word.

Many years later, at 83, Taya was still working, this time at a wardrobe department of a clinic, accepting and handing out clothes. One day an elderly woman came up to her. The woman stared at her, then asked: "Taya, is that you? Do you remember me? I prescribed food for your little grandson. How is he? All these years I have wondered about his health."

Then the doctor cried joyful tears, listening to grandmother's story about her grandson's miraculous recovery, and realizing how she helped change the fate of this young man, now a husband and a father.

Val heard this story from his grandma thirty years after she fed him black caviar; before that, no one had ever talked about it in their family. And two years ago, her adult grandson, who was once sentenced to a life in a wheelchair, ran his first marathon. He ran on his healthy legs, inspired by love and sacrifices made by his grandmother and a kind doctor. A long time ago they both did not give up, so that now he could reach the finish line as a winner.

LIFE LESSON

•

Family is more than just parents and children. An old proverb says: "It takes a village to raise a child." Communes, tribes, and villages are now the thing of the past. Nowadays every family is on their own. This has its own advantages: freedom and independence, unique "rules", and family traditions. But it is not always possible to make it without help. Yet to seek help, one must be humble. Difficulties and disease should not be considered "rubbish" that one should keep tightly under the lid. When the love for our neighbors outweighs irrational thoughts about what others may think or say, love will search, knock, ask, and go the extra mile.

Never give up. Fight for your children to the very end.

In the marathon of life, Love is the only thing that sustains us.

FORGET-ME-NOTS

•

Jesus said: "Ask, and it will be given
to you; seek, and you will find;
knock, and it will be opened to you.

"(Matt. 7: 7-8).

· FAITH ·
Buckwheat for 100 Rubles

In the early 1980's, on the Crimean Peninsula, a large happy family lived in a five-room apartment on the ninth floor of the newly built highrise. The family consisted of a grandmother, Lena, her son and daughter-in-law, and their five children, Faith, Aleks, Elena, Vasily, and Alexey.

The views out their windows were breathtaking; on one side, behind their new apartments, there was a brewery (which didn't look uninteresting to the kids), but behind the brewery stood the forest. In that forest dad and the kids would pick flowers for their mom — the giant red poppies.

Back then Faith, the oldest, thought that the dense forest had no end, there most certainly must have been caves and dugouts there with freedom fighters still living in them. The kids' bedroom window opened to the views of a green meadow that peaked from behind a hillside, and beyond the meadow lay an endless corn field that went on forever. In the summer, their whole city would gather corn there, because everything everywhere belongs to everyone — everything is for the people!*

Faith would collect fragrant thyme in the meadow, and her mother would make the most delicious thyme tea. This place on the outskirts of the city seemed magical, but as soon as they would enter their apartment building, the magic disappeared.

Although the building was new, the porch smelled of trash, the elevator only worked part time, hot water was supplied intermittently, and the lights on the staircase would flicker on and off. Such were the times — unstable and troubled.

Simply providing for their large family was also difficult. Mom would buy food at the market and grow some vegetables on their plot outside the city. One time dad brought home a whole bucket of eggs from the fair, little white eggs all the same size. What a treat! Faith still remembers how much she wanted to count them all.

Sometime after her 9th birthday, a strange and tearful situation happened, leaving a permanent mark on their lives. They never forgot what happened, and remembered it as a good lesson for the future.

Their dad, a hard working provider, worked as the operator

---

* "Everything is for the people" is an old soviet joke. Though the people endlessly labored, they only received a miniscule portion of the harvest; the majority of the bounty went to the government.

of the boiler room, and in his spare time he would do some construction work on the side. He would bring the money to his wife, and she would buy everything they needed. At that time, her father's salary was roughly 170 rubles a month, and that was supposed to feed eight people. Any additional income was much needed to supplement the family's budget.

One day a large bill appeared in their house, 100 rubles! However, it appeared and mysteriously disappeared all on the same day.

The summers in Crimea are brutally hot. Back then soviet citizens had no idea what air conditioning was. To cool their stuffy apartments everyone would simply open their windows, and the flow of air would create a pleasant draft in the room.

That summer, the children's mother was pregnant. Pregnancy was not easy for her. Every day, she and the kids would go up the stairs to the ninth floor, carrying heavy bags of groceries. On that hot day, after a long and hectic search, Faith's mother gathered the children and asked, "Which one of you took the money? 100 rubles have disappeared. "

The kids had no idea what she was talking about. Mom took a crumpled yellow small bill from her wallet, showed it to the children and repeated her question, "Who took a piece of paper that looks like this?" The two little brothers shook their heads. The three older ones, Faith with her brother and sister, also stood in surprise with their eyes wide open. "We didn't take it!" they all said at once.

But their mother would not relent. They didn't have any visitors to their apartment, and she had personally put the bill on top of the refrigerator, but now it wasn't there. "No, my darlings, someone took this money. You just have to give it back to me." After asking, then begging without success and now losing her patience, mother began to scare the children with the belt. "Alright, just wait till your father comes home and spanks you, why are you lying to me?" Dad would have certainly spanked the little thieves, but the money had to be found immediately, so mom had to act on her own.

She began to move the shoes that stood along the wall in the corridor. Then she took out a bag of buckwheat and sprinkled it in a thin stream all along the wall. The children stood bewildered: they had never seen their mother act this way; mother loved to keep a clean house, and here she not only littered, but also threw away perfectly good food! What was she doing?

"Faith, come," mother said and pointed to the buckwheat. The girl obediently dropped her knees onto the groats; the sticky grains immediately dug into her thin knees.

"Aleks, now you." The boy followed the example of his sister without a word.

"Elena", mom gestured to the youngest daughter to stand next to them. The girl was a little cute softie, and she immediately burst into tears from pain.

"Mommy, honestly, we didn't take the money!" they all cried together. Faith can't remember how long they stood there, thirty seconds or five minutes. In situations like this, the time seems to slow down and the punishment feels endless.

Wiping away the tears, one of the children looked towards the kitchen and happened to see the illusive 100-ruble note laying between the wall and the fridge.

The joy of finding the money, earned by her hard working husband, was overshadowed by the bitter regret from her children's undeserved punishment. Perhaps we should leave out how the poor mother, with tears in her eyes, endlessly apologized to her children. The feeling of guilt overwhelmed her, as she realized that it was she who opened the window after putting the money on top of the refrigerator, and the draft simply blew it away.

But no one harbored resentment against their mom, and to this day they do not recall this story with any hurt feelings. On the contrary, what happened on that day would later on help teach them to be considerate without rushing to blame. To become better listeners, to believe their own children, and to ask forgiveness of them.

Parents are not always right. Sometimes, they can make mistakes and be harsh and not because they are evil. In these moments, forgiveness becomes the best fertilizer for sincere love and deeper respect.

Today, their parents are over 60, Faith is over 40, and her sister and brothers are over 30. The babies are now fathers of large families. And recalling this sob story, from time to time, they all still laugh.

And, of course, the whole family still loves buckwheat. Just not on the floor, spilled along the wall, but on a plate served with butter and gravy!

LIFE LESSON

Forgiveness.

Some parents mistakenly believe that by admitting fault or mishap, and apologizing for their behavior, they may lose credibility in the eyes of their children. But in fact, everything is the other way around: good relationships are healed and only become stronger when one asks for forgiveness, while the others wholeheartedly forgive.

Because even when punished unjustly, the pain does not scar the soul when it is followed by explanation and sincere repentance. Children easily forgive mistakes, but they are deeply hurt by deception, hypocrisy, and rudeness.

A great writer Leo Tolstoy wrote, "The children can't be scared away by harshness, but they simply cannot bear lies." No one is able to raise their children without making a single mistake. But the biggest mistake many parents make is that they do not want to admit their mistakes and ask their children for forgiveness.

FORGET-ME-NOTS

•

"...Be kind to one another,
tenderhearted, forgiving one
another, as God in Christ
forgave you."

(Ephesians. 4:32).

· PAUL ·
Croup, Asthma, and Tarsal Coalition

Paul, a healthy, chubby and handsome boy, was born in October 2006. He was admitted into intensive care almost immediately after birth because of fluid in his lungs, and after that he grew weak and frail.

At two and a half he got sick with croup, which brought on serious breathing problems, severe coughing spells, and dark circles under his eyes. In the end the doctors diagnosed the boy with a terrible diagnosis — asthma.

Mom and Dad prayed and worried about their son. At first, the severe coughing attacks would only happen in combination with a cold, but with the onset of fall year after year, they would stretch on longer and longer. Paul's family lives in the Pacific Northwest, where it rains for most of the year with grey, damp weather lasting from October to March. Because of all this rainfall, the landscape surrounding them is incredibly beautiful; the evergreen mountains resemble a thick green fluffy canvas knit with thousands of towering fir trees that are native to this area. But for those who have asthma, this climate is not the best.

Paul's parents persistently asked God for his healing. They kept believing and consulting with their local doctors, as well as their Russian colleagues, and in case of emergency they would use medication — albuterol.

One autumn, after another acute episode, the doctor prescribed steroids for the boy. The instructions were as follows: take every day in the morning and evening. Late at night, when Paul and his sisters were fast asleep, his parents were researching; scouring the Internet and medical forums for the information about this new medication. Paul's mother cried as she read through the long list of side effects, and the terrible stories of parents and their asthmatic children on her screen. After a long conversation, his dad firmly decided, "We will not be giving this medication to our son, but we will pray and believe that God will heal him. Paul will outgrow this asthma."

The boy got older and started school. In late fall and winter, instead of coming to lunch after school he hurried off to lie down on the sofa. He suffered from headaches and the lack of appetite. As a thin and pale child, he would have coughing spells at gas stations, in stores, and especially at night.

The next few years, his parents tried to do everything they knew how. They registered Paul with the Asthma Center in Vancouver, where he was tested for possible allergens. His parents made necessary upgrades to their house; they removed all the carpets replacing them with wood floors, purchased special pillows and blankets, essential oils and diffusers, and much more to no avail.

Then the boy had surgery and his tonsils were removed. Sometimes at the onset of one of his acute episodes, his parents would drop everything and fly the children to sunny Florida or California, but this did not help much. While the girls would joyfully run around and swim in the pool, poor Paul would lay on a deck chair, coughing and wheezing, wrapped with his head in a towel. His mom and dad would fall in and out of despair, pain and tears mixed with sincere hope that everything would soon be better.

A few years later, on Sunday during church service, his mother came upfront and shared her story. She explained how that whole winter, and from then on, Paul managed to cope without steroids, for which they were infinitely grateful to God.

But all this is just a backstory to what happened to the boy between 10 and 13 years of age.

A few years before, his friend Nathan was celebrating his birthday at Sky Zone, a huge building with all kinds of trampolines, every child's dream and favorite place to be. Paul was also invited and excited to go!.

During the party, Paul twisted his ankle, and was carried back home in pain. Keeping in mind that their son's pain threshold was low, his parents didn't take him to the hospital, but rather kept an eye on him for a couple of hours. Closer to midnight, his mother, feeling frantic, persuaded her level headed husband to go to the hospital and do an X-ray, just in case.

After the usual four hour wait and after an exam, they drove home with crutches; there was no fracture, just a twisted ankle. He limped for a little, but quickly got better, and this entire incident was forgotten until their first long hike. Over the next three years, he would periodically complain of pain in that same right foot, and after long walks he would begin to limp again.

Of the three children in the family, he was the middle child. But he was always the first to get tired and always complained of pain, whether at the park, while running, traveling, or any time there was activity. When his mother and sisters would go running, he would ride next to them on his bike. His parents wrote it off as a consequence of that long-standing injury.

Paul was a very kind, sensitive and intelligent boy. In addition to that he was a straight "A" student. In my opinion, that should be enough — not everyone needs to be an athlete. However, at the same time, he was a growing man, which means that he needed to learn how to deal with adversity. When the pain would be too much for Paul to keep moving, everyone would stop, rest, and shortcut the trails, but all the while saying, "Come one son, you are a man. The girls are doing it, so can you! One must press on and persevere in order to be strong." Yet in their heart of hearts, his parents somewhat doubted the prudence of their chosen strategy.

Some believe that being tough on the child will raise a man out of him. But in this case it was never about athletics. The main concern was always health, so, it is what it is, the boy did not like strenuous activity, big deal, it's not for everyone.

Then during his yearly check up at 13, his mom asked the family doctor to examine Paul's foot in order to understand the reason for her son's complaints. That summer he noticed that his right foot did not turn as widely as the left. The doctor wondered why he was not informed about this earlier. Then he felt something unusual in the bones and finally made a diagnosis. Perhaps three years ago there was a fracture, and the bones fused together incorrectly. The doctor made a referral to see the orthopedic specialist, but it took them more than a few days to actually get in to be seen.

After a long wait and a re-examination, this doctor showed Paul's mom a three-year-old x-ray, and was very surprised that his emergency room colleagues did not tell the parents any of these details that night.

It appeared that Paul had a malformation in his foot, tarsal coalition, a common congenital condition. With this pathology, two or more bones fuse together incorrectly while still in the mother's womb.

Back at home, his mom did more research, reading that this kind of bone fusion happens when the process of their development is disrupted at different stages of pregnancy. So, the doctor was right, but no one knew the real cause of this pathology. In addition, the information on this abnormality stated that its symptoms begin to show just between 10 and 13 years of age.

It's unclear why the doctor never said anything about the apparent fusion on the x-ray when it had been taken three years prior. Perhaps he thought that Paul's parents already knew, and the issue at hand was the sprained ankle. Well, thanks be to God! Someone might even think, "It's not even that bad. Surgery can't fix this nor is it needed, everyone just has to learn to keep at Paul's pace."

But that night his mom would not sleep at all.

A good memory does not always serve you well. For hours on end memories flashed before her eyes — family trips, walks, sightseeing, parks and mountains. "Come on, Paul, let's go. Just a bit more, you can do it! You're the man, you are strong! We are all tired too …" All those times he didn't pretend. He was missing cartilage between his bones, his foot was in real pain. Many years ago the little bones fused together, during one of this mother's most difficult pregnancies, when she repeatedly lost consciousness. Not only was it hard on her body but it was also "hard" on his little foot too.

"Forgive me, my son!" the inconsolable mom sobbed. " Lord, forgive me! I didn't know!"

Again and again, the pictures of their travels, walks and hikes, slowly floated before her eyes and drowned her in tears, sinking her with an overwhelming feeling of guilt.

And in another outburst of regret, his mother suddenly thought of compassion while simultaneously realizing that to us much remains invisible. Some pathologies are covered by the flesh, others are hidden deeper than bones and tissues, in the very depths of the heart. We may not know their cause, we may only observe the symptoms, but that does not mean the cause is not there.

LIFE LESSON

•

How does one find a balance between our responsibility of raising a "real man" and indulging ordinary laziness and weaknesses of character? How do you help your child develop strong qualities in himself without breaking his unique qualities? I think we must reject our feelings of guilt and seek God's wisdom. He, as you know, "gives everyone simply and without reproach" (see: James 1: 5).

We need wisdom to understand when to push harder and when to be compassionate, when to be strict and when to be sensitive, and in what circumstance do we discipline the child, or forgive and encourage him.

To put oneself in someone else's shoes, to understand, to sympathize and share in his weaknesses, wisdom is also a must. And only those who clothe themselves in divine mercy, kindness, and longsuffering can bring themselves down to the level of a child.

Most often we learn this from our own mistakes.

For Paul's parents it was important to understand the main task in their situation, they didn't need to make an athlete out of Paul, but they needed to teach him to achieve goals by overcoming himself. Except he didn't have to do it alone, but with his family, with those who are closest to him.

Where there is wisdom, love always triumphs.

FORGET-ME-NOTS

•

"Put on then, as God's chosen ones,
holy and beloved, compassionate
hearts, kindness, humility, meekness,
and patience, bearing
with one another ..."

(Col. 3: 12-13).

· ALEKS ·
Make a Wish

In the mid-1990s, in the freshly dissolved Soviet Union, the borders, as well as the hearts of the people for the message of the Gospel, became wide open. Ministers came from all over Europe and America bringing finances for the needs of the local church. In addition to pastors and Bible teachers, Christian businessmen also came to minister in this vast mission field that was Russia.

Missionaries came to preach the gospel, build churches, and open Bible schools. They brought in huge amounts of money for various projects, sometimes without realizing that the families of the local ministers were in dire need of finances.

However, some of them were worried about the people and were looking for ways to help those in need and their families. Not only did they organize ministries, but also built relationships and made friendships that would span years and decades.

One such entrepreneur from Switzerland first visited Russia in 1992, and he would return every year, sponsoring and organizing Christian camps for children and various crusades. Brother Roland, a blue eyed, unusually kind, and always smiling man visited one pastor's family for several years in a row.

At that time, ordinary people rarely ate out in restaurants and guests were always invited to their house. Roland never came empty-handed; he liked to treat the kids from this large family to exquisite goodies. As a father, he often talked about his own children and always paid special attention to the needs of the local kids.

The pastor's family had a few girls and a young boy Aleks. Maybe it was the over abundance of girly things in the house, dolls, dresses and such, or simply because every boy is like that at his age, but little Aleks really loved cars; not legos, not trains, not airplanes, not even boats, but cars. He knew all the makes and models and would not miss a single one on the road in the hope of seeing some new foreign cars among the usual soviet models and buses.

For him, the best gift was always a new car.

At that time, most children were brought up in modesty; they didn't require extra attention. Back then, one would not see a temper tantrum with screaming and stomping in the toy section of the department store. Back then no one wrote wish lists for Santa, or for their birthdays. Even if the parents would ask their children for their wishes, they most often did not know what to answer.

Modesty is a good quality. Understanding your family's abilities is also important. But what would be even better is a low maintenance disposition, with the ability to dream and even dare.

One day Roland said that his grown son also loves cars. But, real cars, not toys. His dream was a Lamborghini Diablo, but Roland would not allow it because of its terrible name (diablo in Spanish means the "devil.").

On his next visit, the guest asked the parents to call all the children into the room, then he turned to them with a special offer. "I want to fulfill one of your wishes. Wish for anything you like, don't be shy," Roland said with sincerity. The children, confused, looked at each other and at their parents; is this serious or is this a test for greed? After hesitating and smiling timidly they thanked the guest for the offer and said that they didn't need anything.

But Roland would not back down. "Well, tell me, what are you dreaming of? What your parents can't buy for you? The price does not matter. And it doesn't have to be a toy," he explained to the children, and they were completely at a loss for words.

What do children dream about at 10 years of age? They were young, but they already understood the financial capability of this wealthy Swiss man, and their eyes lit up with delight, sorting through the list of " wishes" in their minds. They didn't have the courage to voice their cherished dreams with their parents standing right there, who raised them modestly, thrifty, and altruistically.

The pastor's family lived in a typical three-room "khrushchev" apartment with one hall that also served as the dining room, a living room, and a guest room for all the frequent guests who came to spend a night. It also had two bedrooms, one for the parents and one for the children. In the children's bedroom, with a distance of 5 feet from each other, stood two bunk beds, a wardrobe and a shelf in the corner. The kids didn't know any better, so there was no spacious house somewhere in the suburbs on their "wish list". Oh what a pity, adults would think.

After agonizing with their decision, the children, being encouraged by brother Roland, finally voiced their desires, allowing the generous minister to bless them. The girls asked for rubber bands, hair clips and toys, and Aleks asked for a set of cars. Not a real one of course. Probably those he saw in the store — the ones he really liked.

"Ask, and it will be given to you ..." (Matt. 7: 7).

What will we get? That, what we ask.

It is also written: "... you have not, because you do not ask" (James 4: 2).

But brother Roland also paid for the kids summer camps for that season as well as the next few years. He gave some money to their mother to fulfill the modest wishes of the children.

As a teen, Aleks would recall that incident with regret, "If only I could have that wish now, I would definitely know what to ask for."

Through the years the boy's love for cars only got stronger, by now he had several ordinary and some exclusive automobiles. Perhaps what happened on that day has taught him not only to dream, but dare to fulfill his desires.

LIFE LESSON

•

Today we live in a world of unlimited possibilities and endless choices. But, unfortunately, thousands of young and inexperienced people are irrevocably drowning in the sea of empty ambitions and the pursuit of material wealth. Nowadays, many Christians can hardly separate their sense of success and self-esteem from pathos and pride.

How, then, do we teach our children modesty, at the same time not letting them miss their chance, helping them wisely dare to dream?

Is it even worth teaching?

What if you go too far, and inadvertently make them empty dreamers, fools, or, God forbid, losers and users. Most parents understand that none of this is easy and that it requires a lot of wisdom. It is important to be able to teach the children to accept God's blessings with a humble and grateful heart, but without extremes.

God is good — He is never greedy.

The Lord promises to bless our work and diligence. He promises to help us fulfill His will and the dreams, which He Himself has placed within us. So, we must gratefully accept heavenly gifts and pass them on to others. It is important to learn how to use our talents to become a divine blessing for others — for the benefit of all, but especially our loved ones.

FORGET-ME-NOTS

•

"His divine power has granted
to us all things that pertain to life
and godliness..."
(2 Pet. 1: 3).

· KATIE ·
Mangoes and Flip Flops

Katie is a small, fragile woman with a big loving heart. She is an American citizen, a mother of four children, a Christian, and a wonderful manicurist.

However, thirty years ago, her name was not Katie, but Han Li. She was one of three children in a poor Vietnamese family who lived in a small village in the war-torn and unstable Socialist Republic of Vietnam. The country's leadership blindly tried to copy the Soviet model of the national economy, which led to the devastating economic crisis. Education was not free, so parents had to work hard to give their children at least some kind of education.

Despite the difficulties of life, strict and tough parents loved their children and wished only the best for them.

Because of the warm climate in Vietnam, most everyone wore flip-flops. They were made of either rubber or plastic. The parents would only buy one pair for the whole year, and those who broke or lost them had to walk barefoot the rest of the year.

Although Katie's mom and dad worked very hard, the family was barely surviving. Monday to Sunday, they only ate rice. Once a month an apple was given to the children. In Katie's village tall mango trees grew everywhere, a sweet dream to these poor and malnourished kids. The fruit ripened once a year, but were intended exclusively for sale, and therefore mangoes were carefully protected from insects and various pests. To do this, a paper bag would be placed over each fruit, so the fruit would rippen faster out of reach of birds and worms.

Little Katie's friends were mostly boys rather than girls. She liked to run around the streets, inventing adventures and winning imaginary battles. Her parents often found neatly wrapped empty bags hanging on their trees in place of long-awaited fruits. They knew exactly who had taken them and their thin teenage girl would be punished for disobedience and real damage to the family's budget. But she could not resist, the temptation was just too great.

One day, Katie and her friends discovered unusually large and mature mangoes in their rich neighbors tree, down at the end of the street. Their house was secured with a high fence, and no one covered their fruits with paper bags, the owners did not grow them for sale. The children decided since they were rich, that meant they could share.

The boys came up with a plan and met at dawn the very next day. The branches of a tall tree bent over the fence, if they could throw something at the fruits, there would be no need to venture into the yard. For some reason, the only thing they thought of throwing was a flip-flop.

The boys did not want to risk their shoes, but Katie could not be stopped, her flip-flop immediately flew up, but she didn't throw it hard enough to knock down the large fruits, and her shoe fell far behind the fence — onto the roof.

Goodbye to her only pair!

The kids tried to rescue her flip flop, but instead made a lot of noise, waking the dog and the owners, and eventually running away with nothing.

That afternoon, when her parents returned from work, the neighbor came to complain about their daughter.

"Thief, liar!" her mother yelled, burning with shame. Little Katie was hid under a bed, waiting for her terrible punishment. They whipped her so hard that she still can't forget that nightmare. And she still tells her children that every action has its consequence.

But she remembers more than that.

Katie will never forget how the very next day that same neighbor came to their house again. Who knows, maybe her conscience was bothering her for how severely punished the child was, or maybe she felt sorry for the poor and hungry children, but she brought them several ripe mangoes from her tree, and all absolutely free!

A few days later, dad brought Katie a pair of brand new flip flops. The gesture was so unexpected and, it seemed, undeserved; it made Katie feel loved and cared for. Katie remembers a lot from her literally barefoot childhood, but the story of the flip flop and the mangoes became a manifestation of God's grace and a father's love, which she would encounter again, but only in her new life in another country.

Once, when she was in high school, the students went to a seaside summer camp. Katie did not know how to swim, it was her first time even seeing the sea, but she and the others went into the water. The girl's joy knew no bounds. She stood knee-deep in the water for one second, and after a moment she was already waist-high because of the waves. Keeping her balance was harder. And with a new strong wave, the girl was pulled into the depths. The bottom went from under her, and Katie was under water. Her mind kept replaying one thought: no one is going to help me, I am drowning! She was a Buddhist from birth, but she suddenly remembered her Catholic neighbors and their stories about the good God, who came to people.

In desperation, she mentally turned to Him, "If You are real, save me!" And then she felt a strong hand, pushing her out of the water from under her back. Then everything went dark and silent. When she came to, she found herself lying on the sand, with students and classmates crowding her. "Who saved me?", the girl tried to figure out. They all repeated that they found her alone on the shore. She will never forget the feeling of that strong hand on her back, but, having no explanation for what happened, she simply put that memory on the distant shelf of her memory.

Later, Katie got married, moved to America, and gave birth to four children. She became a professional manicurist and got a job at a salon. Eventually her relationship with her husband broke down and he left them. To provide for her children and to distract herself from depressive thoughts, Katie plunged herself into the work, but the pain would persist, and the feeling of loneliness became even stronger.

Where does one find strength to forgive and to stop living in pain? Who will help her raise the children? Katie's soul was looking for a strong hand on which she could lean on. The answer did not come immediately. But one after another, during a conversation, her clients would tell her about their faith in Jesus Christ. At first she just listened, then she began to ask, "And how do you communicate with God? How does He answer you?"

One time her client, Natasha, invited the Vietnamese lady to her house and offered to help Katie ask Jesus to become her Savior and God. During that prayer, Katie immediately felt His presence. With the overflowing feeling of love, her heart broke and melted. Resentment, pain, and loneliness, and tears were washed away. Suddenly, Katie felt a large, strong hand on her back and immediately was reminded of those terrible seconds under water. It was the same hand of grace that brought her back to life. She accepted Jesus, and with Him, God — a caring and loving Heavenly Father, who became the Father to her children. Now saved by His grace, they live with Him, thanks to her.

LIFE LESSON

•

In Eastern and Slavic cultures, discipline is very important. Some seem to think that being disciplined is a highly spiritual Slavic quality. Perhaps it is partly true, but only if the discipline is applied to oneself.

Nevertheless, the Bible contains an interesting passage, where, oddly enough, it is written that it is not the fear of judgment, but instead, "God's kindness is meant to lead you to repentance." Romans 2: 4.

What a surprise, as it seems that it should be the other way around; harsh rules should discipline us and make us better, and fear of punishment should keep us from sinning.

Every parent understands that without proper discipline it is impossible to raise hardworking, responsible and conscientious children. That is a fact.

But it is also obvious that Scripture cannot be mistaken, which means that our Slavic understanding of constant "army style" discipline does not quite fit with the Lord's plan.

God, our Father, perfectly blends within himself both severity and kindness at the same time. (see: Romans 11:22)

We, as parents, must also develop these same qualities within ourselves: discipline, kindness, gentleness, and long suffering.

FORGET-ME-NOTS

"Therefore, being sober-minded, set your hope fully on the grace..."

(1 Pet. 1:13).

· MARINA ·
A Heart Melting Dress

There is a certain age when older children become almost invisible. Instead, all adult attention is given to babies; how gloriously they smile, which of the parents they look like, and so on, and so forth...

Many people like to be around babies. They are so cute when they babble, so genuinely and wholeheartedly joyful, that it is impossible to take our eyes off of them.

Some people are interested in young adults, as they already have a well developed habit of logical thinking, they have formed a world view, and they can hold a conversation. We are impressed by their youthful passion and at the same time we laugh at their grandiose plans for the future.

But then there are teenagers, they are neither children nor young people, they seem to be stuck somewhere in the middle.

This "layer" of humanity is shy and clumsy, with their arms and legs disproportionate to the body, pimples on their faces, with complexities stemming from this transitional stage and raging hormones. They still don't have a sense of self-confidence, yet at the same time their childlike trust has been erased from their hearts. It is not easy to have a conversation with them. Often they are either completely introverted and quiet, or overactive and aggressive. Sometimes it seems that nobody cares about them, or at least that is how they feel.

Olya was either 12 or 13 years old. She could not say for sure, and her attempts to find pictures in that age range in numerous photo albums of their huge family ended with nothing. Instead, there were hundreds of photos of little Olya. Pictures with bangs and pigtails, with a "boy" haircut, and then again with bangs and pigtails, where she stands with her brother and parents. There were many similar pictures, as well as many first wonderful memories from her early childhood.

And then her younger brothers and sisters were born into the family. Her youngest brother became very ill. He was given a horrible diagnosis — cancer of both eyes. As a result the little boy became blind and died at the age of four and a half.

During that short time, the older children seemed to suddenly mature. They understood everything, no longer required attention to themselves, and tried to help their parents in every way possible. At home they did what they could, praying and believing together with their father and mother. And then they wept, not understanding why, or how, and, most importantly, how were they to live.

Each of them was grieving and worrying about what had happened.

Back then, there were no counselors, nor ministers who could help the children cope with their pain. All they had was their parents, who, in spite of finding no explanations for their own grief, continued to live, love, and believe.

After the funeral, their dad began to have heart problems.

Now the whole focus of the family and their prayers shifted to their dad. All this occurred against the backdrop of constant daily care for their large family, including the babies, and an endless string of household chores.

Even the best and infinitely loving parents can have seasons when their child feels invisible. That's when our merciful Heavenly Father sends His angels into their lives; ordinary people who will pay special attention just to them. They will listen, talk, touch this child's heart, and melt it with the warmth of His divine love.

There are many such angels.

However, in the moment of their visitation we do not understand their true nature. Even decades later the memory of that event is only a small chapter in the story of our life, passing by faster with every year. Sometimes a breeze stirs its pages, and an event, a moment, or a person comes to life again. Then we finally realize the truth of what happened.

One of Olya's angels was Aunt Marina, a quiet, modest, and very kind unmarried young woman. She was not a relative and was about 13 years her senior. Beautiful, slender, immaculate, and always stylishly dressed, Marina came to them from Krasnodon (now Lugansk in Ukraine). Aunt Marina was a talented fashion designer and a skilled seamstress.

During loud church gatherings and family events, when friends came for tea, songs and loud prayers, Marina noticed a clumsy, stooped, and awkward looking teenage girl who was slowly morphing into a young lady.

Marina quietly approached her, sat down next to her, and began talking about something, singling out this girl from adult society. Olya does not remember the essence of their conversations. Perhaps because it was not about anything specific. Olya knew that Aunt Marina made two dresses for her mother, two of her favorites and only outfits, which she would always wear by alternating them .

One day, Marina arrived in a stunningly beautiful dress with cream and brown roses printed on the fabric. It had a collar and ribbons on top, its sleeves were shaped like lanterns, and it was finished with a frill along the hem of the skirt. On its sleeves and at the top of the collar there were inserts in the form of honeycombs gathered by stitches. Against the mundane background of the predominantly gray/black tones of the soviet era, this floral pattern looked like a piece of art.

Olya couldn't even dream of having a dress like this, so she simply admired the dress and asked the designer about how this masterpiece was made.

But Aunt Marina had a habit of talking with God and He, knowing what is in everyone's heart, had revealed something to her that evening. The next time she came to Olya's house, she handed her a bag and said, "This is for you!" When Olya looked inside, she could not believe her eyes, to have such a gift was absolutely unbelievable! She wore that dress to church every Sunday for several years in a row.

In time, her parents recovered, and everything got better. Her mom began to sew again, remaking outfits for her daughters. Then, humanitarian aid came to the former Soviet Union, and the family could now have more and more beautiful outfits. Cooperatives and markets opened up, people began to bring fashionable suits from abroad.

Olya would have many more such beautiful dresses: short and long, black and red, with roses and stripes. Even today she has several dozen outfits hanging in her wardrobe. Olya still loves to wear them all and to share; she puts them on a few times and gives them away to someone.

But unfortunately, Aunt Marina's present wasn't preserved. Yet, as it turns out, Olya wore it in her heart for all of her life! She wore it without even suspecting it, when suddenly a picture of it resurfaced in her memory. But not as a given, not as a fact. It came to life with so many emotions. Only then Olya realized how much she needed that dress, back then at that moment to melt her heart with love and care, to prevent her young soul from becoming stiff and hardened with unanswered questions, fears for dad, bitter resentment, and self-pity.

That thin flowing dress with lanterns for sleeves left a lasting impression in Olya's memories forever.

LIFE LESSON

•

With every passing day our world is becoming brighter, louder, and more visual. Today it is difficult to imagine that not too long ago there were no social networks, and all newspapers, photographs and films were printed exclusively in black and white. This overabundance of information is blinding; we are constantly looking, but seldomly seeing.

Unfortunately, even those who are dearest, closest, and beloved can become too familiar and almost invisible. Like every parent, we hold our newborns with pure joy and trepidation, receiving them as a miracle from above. We look at their peaceful sleeping face with so much delight.

But then they grow. We rejoice at their newfound successes, making marks on the wall, marking their achievements, and celebrating again and again. One day they catch up to us, and they become difficult to handle; each of them becomes difficult in their own way.

Nevertheless, there is a universal remedy that can help every parent survive this difficult stage.

We, as moms and dads of teenagers, need to get as close to our Heavenly Father as possible. We need to literally lean against Him with our whole heart in order to truly understand the Love of the Father; soak it in it with our whole heart and pass it to our children.

Love that is devine is life giving.

This love has the ability to notice flaws, and the roughness of character, and the excess of hormones and, covering those blemishes with itself, it knows how to straighten every imperfection. It can see and warm not only our own children, but even those who are not related by blood. This love can hug the hedgehogs and ugly ducklings and work real miracles by melting hearts.

FORGET-ME-NOTS

•

*"And now these three abide:
faith, hope, love; but the greatest
of these is love."*

(1 Corinthians 13:13).

CONCLUSION

A Second Chance for a Happy Childhood

Unfortunately, we live on a sinful planet where people's childhood is not always happy. But, despite this, our past should not hold us back by overshadowing our lives.

Fortunately, we have God. He heals the brokenhearted, helps us forget our grievances, and frees us from the pain of the past. Figuratively speaking, He removes the thorns from our bouquet of Forget-Me-Nots, our own unforgettable stories from childhood.

We cannot turn back the clock and fix something in the past, or correct mistakes and prevent tragedy. But we believe in the Living God, who sent down His Son, Jesus Christ, to redeem us from sin and death. In Him and by His blood we are cleansed from our childhood disappointments, we learn to love and forgive, just as He loved and forgave us.

The Resurrected Christ is still here with us and He continues His mission of our salvation, reconciliation, and restoration.

This is how the prophet Isaiah describes it,

"The Spirit of the Lord God is upon me, because the Lord has anointed me *to bring good news* to the poor; He has sent me *to bind up the brokenhearted*, to proclaim *liberty to the captives*, and the *opening of the prison* to those who are bound; to proclaim the year of the Lord's favor, and the day of vengeance of our God; *to comfort all who mourn*; to grant to those who mourn in Zion— to give them a beautiful headdress instead of ashes, the oil of *gladness instead of mourning*, the garment of praise instead of a faint spirit; that they may be called oaks of righteousness, the planting of the Lord, that he may be glorified. "(Isaiah 61:1-3, emphasized by the author).

Through redemption, God has given us a second chance , an opportunity to return to our early years, by being part of our own childrens' childhood, so that we can do everything possible to make it a happy one. When we see smiles on their faces, we become immersed into the love of our Creator, and relive the joy of those years that have been lost to us.

But what are we to do with our bouquet unforgettable things? Add to your life's vase only the best flowers, don't hold grudges against your parents, because, be that as it may, they tried their very best and wanted only the best for you. It's time to forgive those who failed at parenting, and not let the weeds prick our hands any longer. After all, we need strong and gentle hands to hug our own children with.

In addition, never forget that God is our Father. He is our perfect and infinitely loving Parent, who supports us more than anyone else, teaching us and setting Himself as our example. In His love we will find strength and wisdom.

Now it is our turn to give life and to raise our own children. Each of them will have their own collection of stories, their own bouquet of Forget-Me-Nots. Will it be made of thorns, or bright colorful memories? In many respects, that is up to us.

What a privilege and what immense responsibility!

We are the makers of their childhoods. And may the words of the prophet Malachi come alive in our lives:

"But for you who fear My name, the sun of righteousness shall rise with healing in its wings… And He will turn the hearts of fathers to their children and the hearts of children to their fathers…" Malachi 4: 2, 6

Forget-me-nots from your childhood

Forget-me-nots from your childhood

Forget-me-nots from your childhood

Forget-me-nots from your childhood

Forget-me-nots from your childhood

Forget-me-nots from your childhood

RELENTLESS

Real stories
of real women
and their
extraordinary
faith

Olya Yarosh

RELENTLESS

Real stories of real women who exhibited relentless faith

Some are the writer's friends and neighbors while others speak to her from the pages of the Bible. Come relive their joys and sorrows, doubts and victories—and perhaps, develop a new perspective on your childhood Bible stories. Like every woman, each chapter is unique and can have a profound effect on your life.

The author discovers for herself and shares with us real life lessons

ABOUT GOD, ABOUT OURSELVES,
ABOUT LIFE AND THE QUALITIES
THAT ASSIST US IN REACHING THE FINISH LINE
BY RELENTLESSLY
OVERCOMING EVERY HARDSHIP.

You can order the book on the website: www.Yarosh.info

www.ingramcontent.com/pod-product-compliance
Lightning Source LLC
LaVergne TN
LVHW012022060526
838201LV00061B/4410

9798349203299